ONLY EVER.

Discovering

Big-Picture Purpose

in Your Daily Journey

*Thank you for all
the support & love!!
Really appreciate it*

04.08.17

Jason E. P. Johnson

ONLY EVER
Copyright © 2017 by Jason E. P. Johnson

Printed in Canada

ISBN: 978-1-4866-1342-7

Word Alive Press
131 Cordite Road, Winnipeg, MB R3W 1S1
www.wordalivepress.ca

Library and Archives Canada Cataloguing in Publication

Johnson, Jason E. P., 1977-, author
        Only ever / Jason E.P. Johnson.

Issued in print and electronic formats.
ISBN 978-1-4866-1342-7 (paperback).--ISBN 978-1-4866-1343-4 (ebook)

        1. Johnson, Jason E. P., 1977-. 2. Christian life. 3. Christian biography. I. Title.

BV4501.3.J669 2016   248.4   C2016-903608-1
                                               C2016-903609-X

To my mother-in-law, Laurie.
You never used the fear of losing your daughter to chase me away.
Instead you prayed for me to find God's way. Your matriarchal
example lives on for me and my family. Thank you.

To my wife, Andrea
You're my dream come true.

To my daughters, Jema and Laurel
You have filled my heart with more love than I thought possible.

CONTENTS

FOREWORD

Jason's passion to see other believers walk in the fullness of the Holy Spirit and experience the reality of the power of God's Word is communicated in this book. I am impressed by the accuracy of the content in light of his own personal walk with the Lord in the ministry of the church and outside of the church.

This is a great motivational, challenging, and life-changing book that brings out simple yet profound truths to take the reader into the realm of walking with God. I enjoy the way he provides a fresh insight and balance of biblical truth along with real, living proof and practical examples. With thirteen years of serving and contributing tremendously to the building of the church of God in the same local church where he was born again, Jason is more than qualified to write on this topic.

This is a must-read for any minister, disciple, and student of the Word of God who desires to have a deeper walk with God in his or her everyday life and be a difference maker in the local church and the world. This inspirational book provides a biblical foundation and practical application for any believer to benefit from. This is a great gift to the body of Christ for our rising leaders and a tool to equip the saints.

—Elhadj Diallo
Senior Pastor
Crosspointe Fellowship

chapter one

CALLED OUT

I had no plans to include what I thought was an outdated God, irrelevant to modern society, in my life. Sure, He created us, but nobody had heard from Him since. God was a cultural antiquity to me.

Nobody invited me to church. I didn't know anybody in the church. Nobody led me through a sinner's prayer. Nobody explained salvation to me. I never attended Bible school. The first (and only) church I tried didn't have a website I could visit to see if I would fit in.

When I heard a voice calling out to me, I was living nearly 1,600 miles away from where I would eventually settle down and meet God.

I felt like an outsider who stumbled in off the street. I chose to become a follower of Christ because of one encounter, to adopt this wild idea and serve Him faithfully in the place where I dedicated my life to Christ and be systematically prepared for the Master's plan.

My life was given away in service to others, and through those sacrifices I discovered my voice to carry God's mandate while striving to keep a tender heart. As I served God in the local church, many of the precepts I adapted were cultivated under another man's ministry through obedience to His word. God used the rippling of ministry to train me to yield to the Holy Spirit, even though I didn't always understand the infinite question of why.

Early on in my new relationship with the Lord, He gave me a taste of His big-picture purpose for my life. It was exciting and empowering. He then asked me to quietly pacify it for thirteen years while building the ministry of the local church as He built me. In this season of my life, my service towards the vision of the church was more essential externally, but the personal calling on my life did not alter. That process is a part of God's purpose in my life.

The same church in which I surrendered my life to Christ is the one that ordained me into the ministry and sent me forth to pursue what Christ predestined me to do. My unpredictable path into God's purpose is an expression of God's heart for people in the worldwide church. The church reaped that which it did not sow directly, adopted me as a brother, then released me and my family back to the Lord as an offering without restraining our global purpose.

This local church cycle is the digestive tract of the body of Christ. All that I required to be equipped to carry the gospel was provided for me in a simple and small but growing church through the guidance of the Holy Spirit. From my perspective, I was unprepared in every way imaginable, but this God I had never met had a plan for me, and He called to me.

A function of every local church should be to receive and stimulate the people of God into their calling. Churches are factories of God-designed destiny administrators, who are compelled and controlled by the Holy Spirit to empower sons and daughters of God to be servants to the world.

God placed me on His assembly line as raw as I could be, to refine me. The only thing I did right was not jump off that conveyor belt until the Master of the factory cleared me for production. Through the church, God was building infrastructure in my life according to His purpose, and the church was building infrastructure around me to support that purpose.

I would not have chosen me. You would not have chosen me. I didn't look or behave like, nor show any proclivities towards, the conventional image of a church attendee.

When I joined my church, it didn't have influence in the city. My church didn't have an outstanding reputation among other churches. It didn't have church plants. It didn't have an amazing facility that met all the needs of the saints.

If I were to have chosen a church that best suited my desires, knowing what I know now, I wouldn't have chosen the one I served in for thirteen years with all my heart. Many people may have that luxury. I did not, because I met God there.

There are many great churches out there, but I cannot speak about them. I have never known another. As a man knows one wife and only shares intimacy with her, I have only ever been with one church to know it intimately.

Everything I required to implement my big-picture purpose was already inside me in the form of a seed that just needed to be planted.

I'm not delivering a pattern to follow, I am only presenting myself as a living testimony. Everybody has their own path with God. My transformed life was all the evidence I needed to believe that God can do all things.

I knew nothing about church protocol. I was green. I didn't know the right words to say. I wasn't familiar with Christian terminology, history, or culture. I was naive to the existence of church politics. I didn't have an agenda to be promoted into leadership, because I never intended to stay. I never thought I was ready for more responsibility, yet God used life trials as an instrument to qualify me. God took me into the deep water to show me His ability to cause me to swim.

I hope to communicate some personal life principles that God has cultivated in my heart through the daily exploration of walking out my faith as authentically as I can; remembering that He has a distinctive purpose for our lives and is actively calling us to come closer to Him so that we may see His plan clearly.

There is always more to God then we imagine. Every day has its purpose and every life has its big-picture purpose in God's perfect plan for all of us.

Whether you find yourself grinding out your faith in your daily journey, or living your days abundantly walking in your big-picture purpose, He is still the *only God ever.*

chapter two

LIFE INTERRUPTED

NOBODY COULD INSTRUCT ME HOW TO FILL THE VOID WE ALL FEEL APART from God, because it was a calling, not a design to be replicated. But I didn't know where to start, so I just began asking around. "What makes you happy? What makes you tick? Who are you? What lets you sleep at night?"

There had to be more to life than having a wonderful spouse and raising great children. Because then what? Wait for the day to return to dust?

I needed more! I needed answers! This deep internal cry allowed me no rest, and I didn't understand what it was or why it was harassing me. Why couldn't anybody help?

As a young teenager, I asked older teenagers, "What makes you happy?"

They introduced me to drugs and alcohol, a trend that would continue until the day I met Jesus Christ. They were only giving me what they knew to escape the emptiness we feel when we have no vision for life.

I was anxious to try the drugs, because I was eager for new experiences. The problem was that I felt like I always had to push harder than everybody else to achieve satisfaction—to engage in the party more than ever, to reach new limits, which led to other bad decisions.

I asked my schoolteachers, "What should I pursue in life to find purpose? To experience greater meaning?"

Their answer was higher education. "It will bring security and you'll find the peace you seek because you will always have a degree to fall back on, and you'll sit at a higher order in the social scale."

I bought in. I worked hard to graduate with two different degrees from two different universities while staying employed to help pay for that education, but I didn't attend either graduation ceremony. I never walked across that epic, triumphant stage.

I didn't want the recognition, because I couldn't deal with the disappointment. Nothing magical happened. I was a student number to the schools, and I felt no achievement because the fire that burned inside me hadn't cooled.

Education wasn't the answer I was looking for, so I became even more restless.

I asked young professionals, who carried themselves with some certainty, "What is it, man? What fills the void?"

Their retort was that you need to be wealthy to find stability. "You'll find freedom in being able to spend what you want, when you want."

I aggressively pursued the American dream, to have lots of disposable income.

For a young guy without financial commitments, I dug in and worked hard. I made some decent money. What I discovered is that it only pushed me further into drugs and alcohol. It left me far more unsatisfied than ever. I put pressure on myself to be the life of every party and to do something even more crazy than the weekend before. Money allowed me to be more irresponsible and prideful.

I gained a reputation for being reckless, and I embraced it. I found myself in and out of drunk tanks, criminal court, getting into fist fights, and having warrants out for my arrest. But internally, I felt ashamed; I had been raised to be a hard-working, morally upright farm boy from the Canadian prairies.

My need for answers became more desperate with each disappointing result. I sought out extreme activity to hide my attempts at feeling normal.

I became fascinated with extreme sports like skydiving, hang-gliding, bungee jumping, and cliff-jumping, because in those moments of intense adrenaline I felt like I was getting close to what would satisfy me. The challenge was that I couldn't free-fall 24/7; even in the plane rides up, I felt the void of an unanswered quest.

I continued asking people who appeared content and were at a different stage in life, "What makes you tick? What makes you wake up in the morning?"

The well-intentioned people would say, "You need to find your soulmate. That one romantic connection that completes you. Then you will find true happiness and satisfaction."

Well, I did meet a girl. This girl was everything I could have asked for. Beautiful, vibrant, intelligent, fun, and innocent. She won my affection instantly, so I decided to make an honest effort with her. We dated for two years and loved each other—at least, with what our understanding of love was at the time. The relationship was intense and enchanting.

However, it seemed we were frustrated at every corner. Something would inevitably happen to cause a setback. Marriage wasn't very important to me at that time because I had no understanding of the intrinsic value of the covenant. So we continued dating with a verbal commitment to each other, but our behavior was unbecoming of our true selves. We finally decided to end the relationship and mutually agreed to remain friends.

It is noteworthy to mention that after two years apart, both of us individually, in different countries, committed our lives to Jesus Christ. In December 2004, we were married. But believe me, that's a story to share another time!

Again I continued asking people, "What gives you hope? What drives you? Is there something more to life than this?"

When I found no immediate inspiration, I sought answers by traveling to different parts of the world, living out of a backpack and having no real concrete plan for the future. I ended up wandering the planet for three years out of that faithful backpack. That was before the days of Google and Facebook. Countries were a lot more unknown. I had email, but most of the people I knew didn't use it, so I still had to use a public payphone every few months to check in with people who cared.

I slept on park benches, in subway stations, on strangers' floors, and basically lived in a van for three months... with two roommates! I found myself in civil riots, government protests, and strange villages that weren't on the map. It was like *The Amazing Race*, only I wasn't competing against other people. I felt like I was competing against my evaporating time in this short life.

I loved the adventure. I enjoyed the unknown—not speaking the language, not knowing a single person, having to figure out the customs and culture quickly in order to get by. I considered myself a student of human nature, intent on reading literary rebels, studying world culture, and engaging in a complicated view of social behavior.

This lifestyle did bring me some small measure of satisfaction, but it was a far distance from the divine answer I sought so desperately.

While in Asia, I would participate in Hindu rituals. I desired more of *something* in my life and was willing to sincerely try new encounters.

I was also influenced by Buddhism during my travels abroad. I read many of the books they shared with me and allowed one gentleman to teach me. I practiced the meditations he instructed. But I never had a defining moment where I could undoubtedly say that I found the explanation I desired to discover.

I had settled in my heart that these travel adventures must be what I was meant to do. I was out of ideas. I had no fresh inspiration to pursue, nothing to bring a deeper meaning to my life.

When I ran out of money, I came back to North America and took a job just outside Los Angeles, California. My ambition was to make this my home for six months of the year, so I could surf in my free time and spend the remaining six months wherever my instinct took me. My attitude was "I'll do whatever I want, whenever I want to do it."

It's not that I was content in life, it's that I had settled. The unexplainable desire I'd had since my youth made me very cognitive of its presence—or should I say, its absence. I longed for more, but had no resolve left to seek it.

It was like I could always hear beautiful music but could never discover the source. The closer I got, the clearer the sound; the farther I ran, the more muffled the sound became. But it never stopped playing.

This force pushed me beyond my years into experiences that would shape me into the man God custom-designed me to be.

While I was living in Redondo Beach, I woke up in the middle of the night to the sound of a voice. I sprang up and opened my eyes to check the time. To this day, I can't tell you if the voice was audible or if I heard it in my head—it happened too fast—but the voice told me to go to Calgary, Alberta. I immediately went back to sleep in peace, and in the morning I decided that whatever the voice had been, I was going to follow it.

I dismissed it as my instinct, my free nature choosing a place for me to seek adventure. It's not like the voice was so overwhelming that it left me no choice. It wasn't thunderous. It didn't paralyze me. It only seemed to beckon me with calm assurance. In retrospect, I certainly didn't understand that God was calling me out.

I didn't leave immediately. I actually went to South America first, and then eventually found my way up to Canada, not really knowing why I was going anyway. I had never needed a reason to travel though, so this was no different.

I arrived in Calgary looking for life experience, like I had done so many different times in other parts of the world, but not expecting much. After all, it was a familiar country to me and I didn't intend to stay. My thought was to remain eight months and then head up to Alaska for a fishing job I had lined up.

In the neighborhood I lived in, I discovered a small, retro-looking church and every week I passed it several times on my way to the gym. I vividly remember the rumble of my old '73 Volkswagen Kombi van as I sat at the intersection waiting for the red light to turn green. I often looked over to the church, noticing nothing significant about the building. It was not aesthetically impressive, but for some strange reason I found that appealing. It was like I began a relationship with a building, greeting it every time I drove by.

One day, as I drove past it with my friend, I declared, "If I ever try a church, I'll try that one right there." After announcing my thought, it became all I could think about. The following day, while driving my typical route, I noticed a sign outside the church advertising a guest speaker on Friday night. Normally my friends and I would go to the clubs, but on this particular night I dropped out to go try that little church.

My friends weren't surprised that I wanted to try something new, so it was no big deal to them—but they weren't interested in coming with me either.

Walking into a scene alone, without anyone to guide me, wasn't unusual for me. I didn't feel uncomfortable, though this night would forever change the course of my life.

My initial impression as I entered the church was with a nod of approval and the thought "oh cool, a live band." At least that's what I called the worship team because that church terminology was foreign to me. I found a seat near the back. I wasn't interested in meeting people, only hoping to understand what had drawn me to this place.

The preacher got up and preached a word. I had no understanding of it. It went over my head, but he did say at the conclusion that he was going to pray for anybody who wanted to be prayed for. He requested that we form a line and he would go through to pray for us.

I was open to the thought of someone praying for me. I had let lots of people pray for me, people from many different religions in case it would help me find the answer—or even a clue—to the questions that had intensified in me ever since childhood.

The gentleman approached me as the music played. I noticed others reacting to his prayers with different expressions. Some even fell over or chose to sit or lie down. As for me, I decided that I wouldn't fall or lie down. That seemed a little much for my first time. I told myself simply to listen to his prayer and then go home for the night.

I braced myself by putting my legs in a defensive position, just to make sure the preacher didn't push me over.

When the preacher touched my head to pray, he never got a word out. At least, none that I audibly remember. I immediately dropped to the floor.

On that floor, in the back of this small church, in an unfamiliar city, not having even one acquaintance with me, I was introduced to the Almighty God in an instant. I lay motionless for I don't know how long as He began to answer my questions and show me things about my life and the lives of the people around me.

It was too profound to imagine and too vivid to deny. God revealed Himself to me!

When I arose, I sat in a chair that wasn't mine as prayer ministry carried on. I picked up a Bible that didn't belong to me still in awe of what was happening to me. I hadn't brought a Bible, because I didn't know that people actually brought Bibles to church.

While on the floor, God had showed me a scripture out of the book of Job, but I wasn't sure it was a scripture because of unfamiliarity. I anxiously flipped through the entire Bible, because I didn't know where the Book of Job was, or if it was in the Bible at all. I vaguely recalled a spy movie I had watched a few weeks earlier, *Mission Impossible*, in which one of the clues to the mystery had been a verse from Job.

Well, I found it. This verse was the concluding statement to all the imagery God had revealed to me in that time on the floor. The power of God captured me that night and His Word fortified what I had just experienced. With tears streaming down my face, I declared to God in a whisper, "Now that I know You are real, I will serve You the rest of my life!"

In recollection, I see that it was my first prophetic statement.

Nobody explained to me that I had to be born again. Nobody asked me any questions, or steered me into recognizing myself as a sinner, but I knew when I got up off the floor that I belonged to God. He embraced me as His own.

I recall seeing a polite, well-dressed church lady who I'd made eye contact with before the meeting. I grabbed her by both shoulders and shook her enthusiastically while shouting, "God is real!"

Instead of fear gripping her, she began to weep. "I know, I know," she replied as we both sobbed.

My life was no longer my own. The understanding I had longed for had appeared in an instant. I was overwhelmed. I felt energized about life, and the most fascinating part is that I instinctively knew there was more. It was like discovering a well in a dry land; the water was so fresh and sweet, and I thirsted for more!

I couldn't get enough.

There was a weekly small group meeting that I attended in the basement of that same little church. I ate mandazi (African donuts) and listened to a gentleman passionately preach. I found myself singing, "There is power, power, wonder working power in the blood of the lamb."

I realized later just how much I needed this group to discover God intimately, and myself spiritually.

Because of the size of the small group, I had the opportunity to augment my heart through servanthood to facilitate the meetings. All positions were vacant, so I immediately began helping in any way I could. I would arrive early, tidy up the area, set out chairs, bring the pulpit from the main sanctuary to the basement, and assist in organizing food in the kitchen. I would sit in the front row to catch everything being spoken and encourage the speaker with a good Pentecostal "Amen" or "Preach it."

During ministry times, I attended carefully to the speaker, stretching my hands out and believing with them in prayer. After the meetings, I served food and followed up with everybody present to discuss what had been preached. I would hang around after to clean, lock up, and give people rides home. Or I'd head off to the all-night diners to continue the discussion.

It was a new world to me because it was a new life. Old things had passed away. I couldn't change my past, but I *could* change the way I looked at it. I traded my shame for God's shaping.

I cultivated my heart in relationship with our Heavenly Father. I grew up in that same local church, serving wholeheartedly with every ounce of passion under His care. I was thoroughly engaged in building the corporate God-given vision for thirteen years knowing full well that I had been designated to do a different type of work for the Lord in the future.

As we grew from a small group in the basement to a well-respected assembly with several church plants, both national and international, from the grassroots, I also grew.

I had heard a voice. I had made the choice to follow that voice. I hadn't known who or what God was, but that didn't stop destiny from sounding the alarm that my time had come to live for Jesus. He gave me life and a purpose. He found me where I was. He called me according to His good plan. He still satisfies me to this day.

chapter three

DESTINY HAS A VOICE

I$_N$ MY QUEST TO DISCOVER THE DEEPER MEANING OF LIFE, I COMPLETED FIVE
years of university as a full-time student. I worked all summer and many
evenings to pay for my education, but still had looming student loans. I
was then employed in my field of study for two and a half years before
God invited me into full-time ministry. My wife and I were newly married and we had just purchased our first home together.

Few people agreed with my choice to leave the secure salary and
benefit options offered by having a college degree to pursue my divine
calling. It did appear impractical, but I was compelled to obey and let
go of that security in order to discover what was waiting for me in
God's plan.

When I was a young skydiving student, trying to work my way up
in number of solo jumps, I recall being on a plane with another student
jumper who was about to make her first jump. The mind can play funny
tricks on a person when it can't make sense of what the body is about
to do, especially if the action is impractical.

On the plane there were three students, a pilot, and somebody
called the jump master or instructor. It was soon the girl's turn to move
out onto the support bar that is attached to the wing of the plane, hang
by two arms, let go, and move into the arch formation. Understandably,
she was having second thoughts and expressed it to our jump master.
Our jump master tried to motivate her by shouting adrenaline-laced
words, but they seemed to shake the student even more.

The jump master then tried some different psychology by yelling profanities and demanding that she get out on that wing. Now she was adamant that she wasn't going to jump. At last, amidst the awkward sound of empty air moving through the cabin, she agreed to make the jump, but only if the instructor would come with her. The instructor agreed immediately.

He put his hands on the back of her hands and together they waddled out onto the wing. With both of their hands on the support bar, her feet moved off the floor out of the cabin. His did not. Her entire body weight was now outside the plane. The jump master then moved back inside the plane and gave a cheeky little wave, knowing that the student jumper would eventually let go. All student jumpers use a pilot shoot that opens automatically. It was just a matter of time before she was forced to deal with the inevitable and let go of the support bar that she was so preciously holding onto. She did ultimately let go, and her pilot shoot did open.

On the ground, the jumper was ecstatic with her experience. She ran over to the jump master and gave him a leaping hug as a thank you. That student could have missed the experience of a lifetime, but the deception of man tricked her into it. The jump master had seen this scenario a hundred times.

How many more times has God seen His creation have to let go and trust that He knows the result?

God can be persistent, but never deceptive. Our jump master Jesus doesn't deceive or demand; He simply appeals. In regards to our destiny, we know generally what we're getting into. Purpose is present deep down in the depth of our hearts. Perhaps not all the details, but we understand the theme.

> *[H]e predestined us for adoption to sonship through Jesus Christ, in accordance with his pleasure and will... In him we were also chosen, having been predestined according to the plan of him who works out everything in conformity with the purpose of his will...*
> —Ephesians 1:5, 11, NIV

Destiny is hardwired into us. We cannot run or hide from the Spirit of God because no matter where we go, there He is! We could submerge ourselves at the bottom of the ocean in hope of escape, but there He would be. We can propel ourselves out of the atmosphere, but even then we would not be out of God's reach.

Destiny isn't chance or being in the right place at the right time. Destiny has a voice. Destiny is God's pursuit of a surrendered life ready to collide with His purpose.

In Matthew 4, Jesus was water-baptized and tested in the wilderness, and He hadn't claimed to be the Son of God or performed one supernatural miracle yet.

> *As He was walking by the Sea of Galilee, He noticed two brothers, Simon who is called Peter and Andrew his brother, throwing a dragnet into the sea, for they were fishermen.*
>
> *And He said to them, Come after Me [as disciples—letting Me be your Guide], follow Me, and I will make you fishers of men!*
>
> *At once they left their nets and became His disciples [sided with His party and followed Him].*
>
> *And going on further from there He noticed two other brothers, James son of Zebedee and his brother John, in the boat with their father Zebedee, mending their nets and putting them right; and He called them.*
>
> *At once they left the boat and their father and joined Jesus as disciples [sided with His party and followed Him].*
>
> —Matthew 4:18–22, AMP

When our time has arrived to be appointed into our big-picture purpose, God comes looking for us! It is not us looking for God.

Peter didn't notice Jesus walking by. Jesus noticed him! God already knew the disciples and knew where to find them. God had predestined them to be the disciples of Jesus, and they would turn the world upside-down. Destiny had already chosen them. They were doing what they had always done: working their day to day jobs, but Scripture says they immediately left what they knew and answered a voice that called out for them.

Practically, it makes no sense, but the new disciples must not have heard a human voice. They heard the voice of destiny, God's voice through the man Jesus Christ, and they responded in obedience, activating their destiny and purpose. There must have been something about this voice that sounded different, some internal reaction that awoke an innate eternal calling.

Elisha was plowing a field with oxen when the prophet Elijah called out to him. Elisha didn't ask Elijah if he could follow him. Elisha didn't seek him out or go out to meet Elijah. Elijah found him. Elisha kissed his mother and father goodbye, slaughtered his oxen, and burned his plowing equipment. There was no turning back for Elisha. Elijah even attempted to convince Elisha to turn back, as if to say "I wouldn't choose you," but Elisha had determined in his heart to serve God regardless of another person's opinion.

The prophet Samuel was instructed by the Lord to go to Jesse of Bethlehem and anoint one of his sons to be king of Israel. This wasn't Jesse's idea. It wasn't even Samuel's idea, but there he was among all the sons of Jesse except one. The prophet of God thought to choose Eliab based on his appearance, but God reminded him that He doesn't choose based on what's visible; rather He chooses based on what's invisible.

Jesse had seven of his sons pass before Samuel, yet God had rejected them all for this position. The eighth son, David, wasn't even in the room. He was such a long shot, the least likely among his brothers. But Samuel used the voice of destiny and said, "Send for him. We will not sit down until he arrives." The honoring of a king had already begun, even though David was just a shepherd boy to his community and family.

David didn't arrange his schedule to make sure he was present on the off-chance that Samuel might consider him to be king of Israel. David was out tending sheep for his father. David was sought out by the Spirit of God and invited to where he needed to be to fulfill his destiny.

The risen Lord called out to Saul the persecutor, even though he was in hateful opposition to Christ. Saul was on the road to Damascus, intending to visit the synagogues to rally support to terrorize more Christians. He was en route to make life miserable for the followers of

Christ when the risen Jesus found him. Destiny interrupted Saul and caused a fierce opponent of the gospel to become a most willing servant.

Destiny seeks out the called. God will find us when our time has come to move into a different dimension of His purpose for our lives. In the meantime, we cultivate obedience through servanthood to nurture our calling. The disciples served the crowd. Joshua served Moses. Elisha served Elijah. David served King Saul. Saul the persecutor became Paul, a bondservant of Christ. Jesus served the world. While we remain in this role of serving, the voice of God will cut through all the exterior noise and plans of man to alert us to destiny.

After I surrendered my life to Christ, I took romantic relationships far more seriously as a single guy. I felt like I would only get one chance to do it right, so I focused more attention on my relationship with God rather than searching high and low for a suitable wife.

Somewhere deep down in my heart, from the day I first met her I wanted to marry this woman of God named Andrea. But I never had the courage to pray for her to be my wife. Frankly, I was afraid God would say no. I was a young Christian, so I dismissed her as a possibility and did my best to forget about her for almost two years.

Until one day, the voice of God interrupted my praises to Him and spoke vividly to assure me that Andrea would join me. I was instructed to keep doing what I was already doing. I was told to continue encouraging her and lifting her up in the Lord. God was telling me to trust His plan even when I was lying to myself about how I felt.

God had a plan for us to be together. I was reluctant to believe it. In my head, I had ruled her out as impossible, but when God revealed to me His knowledge for my life, it set me free and emboldened me to pursue her with confidence in a pure way.

Before you can ask God what to do, you must know who you're asking. God wants us to live by discernment or revelation knowledge. To live by revelation is to not live by information. When we ask God the hows and whens, we are requesting information so our faith doesn't have to operate fully trusting in the Lord. God uses this method because information doesn't change us, but revelation does. Intellectual pride will never draw us closer to Him; it will only prepare us for a fall. Logic doesn't save us from hell; the revelation that Jesus is the Christ does.

Destiny submits to the will of God, who authored a custom destiny for each of us.

We feel the calling but desire more detail before we're willing to step out. So we ask God what we should do with our lives, but God doesn't often respond with perpetual daily instructions of "do this" or "do that." We're looking for information to avoid the discomfort of walking by faith. We feel anxious, like we're wasting time, or fearful that we'll make a wrong choice and miss the will of God. So we make no choice at all, forfeiting our delight in exploring who God is. We become aloof from God through the fear of choosing wrongly, but this is what causes our anxiety. Purpose is full of process, yet we prepare more for days of comfort than we do days of destiny. God isn't afraid of the process, and neither are people who are close to God relationally.

God doesn't work like that. He let Adam and Eve disobey Him and eat the fruit of the Tree of the Knowledge of Good and Evil, even though He knew it would later cost Him His only begotten Son. Could God not have intervened?

He is merciful, gracious and confident to let all mankind choose right or wrong.

We can cultivate our trust in God's destiny for us while we're in the holding tank. What we do on any given day does not always look like the perfect plan that God has laid out for us. God is greater than our destiny. If we discover our destiny before learning to trust in the Lord, we run into confusion. That's why God would prefer we seek Him rather than ask, "What should I do?"

A French writer once wrote that if you wish to build a ship, don't divide the men into teams and send them to the forest to cut wood. Instead teach them to yearn for the vast and endless sea.

God could instruct us step by step, and undoubtedly those who love Him would obey. We would live our lives never yearning for the endless depth of an infinite God. There would be no spiritual hunger and very little discovery of what God is capable of doing through us.

We wouldn't have the honor of partnership, but instead be employees working by the hour, looking for shortcuts so we can go home early.

That's why we only get little tastes of destiny at a time, to protect the intimate relationship. It's not punishment for not working hard enough, or remediation for bad decisions. We will stop seeking when we think that we can go no farther. It is we who have limitations, not God. It's so that we can achieve our destiny God's way for His glory!

We won't stop yearning for destiny until we find ourselves in heaven at the feet of Jesus. So while we're here on earth, in these bodies, we pursue the absolute truth through our intimate relationship with God. Let God handle destiny according to His pleasure and will for our lives.

When you fly somewhere, you often get to know the person you've been seated next to during the flight. You don't get to know them once you've arrived at your destination; communication and knowledge are exchanged during the trip. Is that not why we date before we get married? If marriage is the destination, don't we want to get to know who we'll spend our lives with? There is a season of intimate communication before committing to one another in eternity. Is Jesus coming back for His bride, the church? Should He not desire to get to know us before the marriage supper?

God wants us to discover who He is apart from what we can do for Him and what He can do for us. Performance is never a requirement. How could that be true love? True love is unconditional and sacrificial.

> *For His divine power has bestowed upon us all things that [are requisite and suited] to life and godliness, through the [full, personal] knowledge of Him Who called us by and to His own glory and excellence (virtue).*
>
> —2 Peter 1:3, AMP

"All things" flow out of our personal knowledge of Him who called us. Ministry, purpose, provision, husbands, wives, children… all become illuminated to us through an intimate understanding of who God is. Relationship causes us to change our hearts to reflect the heart of our Father. Our thoughts become like His thoughts.

"All things" don't change our relationship with God; our relationship with God changes "all things." How we respond to God when we want something is how we will respond to God when we have something. He wants us to have knowledge of where our hearts are as human beings, and where His heart is at as God in any circumstance He puts us in. This exchange is a form of personal communication from God to man.

We've got to be plugged into the Source through relationship. A lamp that's not plugged in has no power. It just *looks* like it should have power from the outside. A lamp with no power never gets used for what it was designed for. Sadly, it never fulfills what its intended purpose was.

Have you ever had a stranger ask you for money? Whether or not you choose to give, you'd probably be startled by the request. Why? Because you don't know them. They expect a no for the same reason. How could a person submitting a personal request really feel confident asking a stranger for anything?

When we are confident, we can believe for the impossible while it is still unseen. Belief leads to behavior. Everything has a spiritual component. A person can tell what you believe (spiritually) based on how you behave (physically).

Confidence in Christ doesn't come through the blessings of God or our ability to perform by the gifts God gave us. Confidence comes through our relationship with Him, because we know Him and He knows us.

Sometimes we base our relationship with Jesus on how much we love Him, as though our actions will prove to Him our love. However, the grace of God structures our relationship with God based on how much He loves us. That assurance reminds us that this life is more about God than us.

Proverbs 3:26 says, *"For the Lord shall be your confidence, firm and strong, and shall keep your foot from being caught."* (AMP).

If we tend to our relationship with Him first, He will take care of our ability to hear the voice of destiny. That developed confidence accustoms us to trust His plan despite the outward appearance. Our calling becomes loud and clear to us. He has more at stake than we do. After all, He seeks us out before we start looking for Him.

chapter four

THE WAGE SERVANT AND SHEPHERD

WHAT IS LIFE ON EARTH REALLY ALL ABOUT? IS THERE SOMETHING MORE meaningful than belonging to a wonderful family or finding a great church?

Do we need to experience nature, culture, and world travel to attain human knowledge? To somehow connect with mankind so we won't be left feeling isolated and misunderstood? Are we to pursue our desires with intense focus to receive the world's vague promises of a good life and the fading reward that leaves us with unsatisfied disappointment?

Why do we wander the earth in search of meaning? Intellectuals, scholars, poets, and artists can express this, but every person who breathes thinks about it. Are we to leave this mortal body and transition into the unconscious never to produce another emotion, thought, or expression? There has to be a greater sense of purpose in this life, or why submit to any authority or morality?

Jesus said that *"the Son of Man came not to be waited on but to serve, and to give His life as a ransom for many"* (Matthew 20:28, AMP). He came not to be served, but to serve others. He illustrated heaven's model of servanthood. Along the way to His big-picture purpose on the cross, He served. Jesus knew what His mission was, and as He lived out the perfect timing of God, He gave His life away in service to others. This is our example to follow.

The most secure route to fulfilling our purpose is through the acts of a servant. Many people know that Jesus came to earth to die on the cross for mankind, but we often overlook the first part of His own sentence—that He came to the earth to serve. Genuine service draws us close to God and keeps us safe. Servanthood makes sense of life and helps format the purpose of God in our lives.

As long as we have an unclear direction in life, we become increasingly tired, frustrated, and disgruntled. It's difficult to be passionate about something we're confused about. In that state, it is much easier for us to slip away into the monotonous, slumbering lullabies of the evil one, satan. He sings songs that inspire false doctrine, distraction, deception, and apathy. Some of his greatest ballads include "It's all about me," "I'm not good enough," and "God doesn't really care anyway." These repetitive slogans gently sway us into selfishness, complacency, and idle pursuits that produce vain, meaningless disappointments. Satan's intention is to lead us down the broad path of destruction through deceptive messages and partial truths of lust and pride to provoke us to lack self-worth and a true identity.

We all know that the thief comes only in order to steal, kill, and destroy. Nobody would take advice from somebody with a reputation like that unless the message was subtle and consistent enough. Satan uses these doubts to combat our self-affirming beliefs. After describing the thief who comes to steal, kill, and destroy, Jesus describes Himself as the Good Shepherd who lays down His life for the sheep (John 10:10–11). The scripture draws a stark contrast between the thief and the Good Shepherd.

John 10:12 introduces a third character referred to as the hired servant. *"But the hired servant (he who merely serves for wages) who is neither the shepherd nor the owner of the sheep, when he sees the wolf coming, deserts the flock and runs away"* (AMP).

The hired servant is a reflection of people who serve by the hour, people who give their time but only up to a limit of their choosing. These hourly service people will serve if their conditions are met. They often serve from a sense of obligation, guilt, or religious duty. Hired servants are concerned about how they will be remediated for their service. They usually don't understand the vision or mission of the company or church as a whole, and at the first sign of discomfort they will abandon their post and look for another place to be employed or serve. They will do little to cause an increase in profit for their employers, or do little to grow the church.

John 10:13 says, *"Now the hireling flees because he merely serves for wages and is not himself concerned about the sheep [cares nothing for them]"* (AMP).

Earlier in that same chapter, Jesus says, *"But he who enters by the door is the shepherd of the sheep"* (John 10:2, AMP). In John 10:9, Jesus declares that He is the door, and implies all those who enter properly will behave in a successive manor to the Good Shepherd.

When we enter the sheepfold or become followers of Christ, it must be by one door only, and that is the revelation that Jesus is the Messiah. The superlative shepherd of the sheep is Christ, and if we are to imitate the Good Shepherd, we must lay our lives down in sacrificial service for the sheep.

True servants reflect their Savior and shepherd the sheep. Their concerns are for other people more than their own gains. They put the needs of others in front of their own, voluntarily. Servants operate with increase on their lives because of their faithfulness. They live in the abundant life that Jesus promised in John 10:10.

Christianity needs to be demonstrated. Jesus Christ the Son of God showed Himself in the flesh to authenticate the Father. In John 10:18, Jesus says, *"These are the instructions (orders) which I have received [as My charge] from My Father"* (AMP).

True servants look, sound, and act like their Father. They shepherd the sheep. Servant-hearted people don't sacrifice to exhibit who they are; they sacrifice to display whom they belong to, and that is the Good Shepherd.

> *Whatever may be your task, work at it heartily (from the soul), as [something done] for the Lord and not for men...*
> —Colossians 3:23, AMP

Amid our commitments, we will undoubtedly be tested in our service to identify whether our hearts are that of a hired servant or someone who shepherds the sheep. Those tests are for us to identify where our motives are for servanthood. It is a way God communicates the condition of our heart to us.

Why do you think the Department of Transportation makes you take a written exam before you attempt the in-car driver's test? To evaluate where you're at. If you don't pass the written exam, you go home, make some adjustments, work at it a little more, and come back to retake the test. When you have successfully passed, you and the governing authority know that you're prepared for the driver's test.

Put me on trial, Lord, and cross-examine me. Test my motives and my heart.

—Psalm 26:2, NLT

The test is there to provide tangible proof that our service is genuine. God understands that our human nature and logic make it difficult to believe in the unseen, so we need verifiable evidence through trial for God to communicate to us where our true heart is at. Difficult circumstances in our lives test where the invisible strengths and weaknesses reside within us.

Paul, the bondservant of Christ, wrote to the churches from prison in Colossians 4:17, *"See that you discharge carefully [the duties of] the ministry* and *fulfill the stewardship which you have received in the Lord"* (AMP).

Let's dissect this statement. The word *fulfill* can be described as to succeed in achievement, to fill to full, and to satisfy completely all the requirements necessary.

Stewardship is the management of resources. All resources come from the Source, but it is the administration of these possessions that reveal the heart of man. What do you do with your time, money, and talents? How do you disperse them? How do you increase them? Every resource at our disposal—whether in thought, will, or action—should conform to service for the Lord to advance the Kingdom of God.

What ministerial duties have we received in the Lord? "In the Lord" suggests that dominion belongs to the Lord. When we are *in* another country, we are subject to its laws. The country owns the land, so when we are allowed to enter, we are to submit to the ruling authority.

We acknowledge ourselves as subordinates to the country at customs upon entrance and exit through a declaration card that we provide to the representing officer.

Likewise, we will give an account one day about what we received "in the Lord" during our time on earth. The earth is the Lord's and the fullness thereof. He is the Creator and Sustainer of people, so He really owns the human race. He gave us the breath of life and decides when there will be no more breath left in us. We have received the responsibility of stewardship for our own lives.

There is a difference between ownership and stewardship. If I were to borrow my friend's cell phone, even though it was in my possession, I would not own it. In fact, if you called the phone looking for my friend you would be suspicious of me answering, and certainly taken aback by my unfamiliar voice saying hello. I would be responsible for that phone while it was in my possession, but that wouldn't mean I had ownership of it by default. I would have to give an account to the rightful owner when I turned possession back over.

God has trusted mankind with the earth and trusted us with stewardship of our lives. God designed the big-picture purpose for us as individuals, allowing us to make personal choices. God will hold each of us accountable for those choices. In order to fulfill our stewardship role, we should realize that we are part of a bigger plan and purpose than how we arrive at death. Our God-given purpose is not to arrive at death safely and comfortable. Remember, Jesus Christ came to serve, and He died uncomfortably on the cross. We must recognize that we are given opportunities in life to serve and be a contributing partner in the Kingdom of God.

I have stood in rooms where a person knows she is dying, and never in such a situation have I been a part of a conversation about increasing wealth. All pride melts away and the essence of human life remains, sobering the atmosphere. Nothing is funny. Every word matters, as it may be their last.

The intensity reminds me of how Oskar Schindler was depicted in the movie *Schindler's List*. Schindler is credited with saving 1,200 Jews from Nazi persecution during World War II. At the end of the war, he deeply lamented that he had not done more with his resources to save people.

I grew up on the Canadian prairies in the middle of nowhere, about fifteen kilometers from the closest village. That village contained approximately 450 souls, if you count goats. I lived on a large farm, and one of my first responsibilities was to close in the chicken house doors at night to protect them from predators such as coyotes. I was about five years old when my parents began testing my stewardship. I understood that I had a responsibility to watch over these chickens for the sake of the family's welfare. If I failed, my parents would suffer loss and there would be less prosperity for the family. Worse yet, my parents might not be able to trust me with more. I couldn't read or write, but I could comprehend responsibility. I understood that I was making a contribution to a bigger operation. I had the innate ability to see the bigger picture.

God has custom-designed us so that stewardship is built into our human functionality. We are project managers for the business of our Father. Our seemingly small acts of service are part of a much bigger movement.

Why do you suppose the enemy spends so much time trying to convince us to be lazy, unmotivated, difficult to work with, apathetic, and uninvolved? He wants us be distant from the body of Christ, aloof in our relationship with Christ, insecure and self-abasing around other members. Satan would prefer that we be too proud to lower ourselves for certain tasks, that we be too reserved and serious to help in the kitchen or children's ministry. After all, service in those ministries isn't seen by people.

Now, a person may think closing in the henhouse at night is an easy task for a young lad, but it came with some challenges. Chickens don't go inside until after dark, and good luck trying to herd chickens inside before that point. Also, you don't raise chickens next to the house because of the smell and noise, so naturally you move them as far away as possible. To a child, this area was like a no man's land. Sure, it was still on our property, but I had to walk far from the house, in the pitch dark, through long grass, amidst the background noise of wild coyotes close enough to watch me shut the chickens in every night.

If I had known scripture as a kid, I would have recited, *"Yea, though I walk through the valley of the shadow of death..."* So I equipped myself with a flashlight and a belief in order to make my task achievable. I convinced myself that if I met a coyote, I could run faster out of fear than he could out of hunger!

I could shine the flashlight toward the chicken house, but the light covered such a large area that it dimmed my perception of the destination. If I kept my light on the destination, it didn't make my steps any safer, because I still couldn't see what was directly in front of me. I also had to proceed very slowly, because I felt unsure of my footing.

However, since I knew the approximate location of the chicken house, even in the dark, I could simply head in that direction and shine the light in front of my feet to provide a much clearer view—and I would arrive at my target much faster, and more safely. The trick was to take small, quick steps with the full power of the flashlight directly in front of me. And every once in a while I would stop, look at my destination, adjust my direction, and continue on.

> *Your word is a lamp for my feet, a light on my path.*
> —Psalm 119:105, NIV

The fulfillment of God's destiny requires the same strategy. God has a purpose in mind for us and we have a general idea of what it is. Take small steps of servanthood, illuminated by obeying His Word, and you'll arrive safely at your destination in His perfect time. If you have to stop for a moment to adjust direction and remind yourself where you're going, the pause will not change the destination.

The essence of servanthood isn't established by what we're able to do, because we need to show God how much we love Him. The measure of servanthood is in how much we accept His love for us. Therefore, service isn't provided by human ability or energy alone, but by understanding and faith. There are people in our community who serve for different reasons, and then there are servants who shepherd the sheep.

The heart of a servant comes from understanding who God is and what He has already done for us. Servanthood correlates with our personal knowledge of Christ. The love of God, the grace of God, and the righteousness of God don't need to increase in our lives for us to be able to have a servant's heart. Our *belief* of its existence, and our *acceptance* of it, needs to increase. That understanding of God's love, grace, and righteousness will encourage us to give all we can for the benefit of mankind daily, just as Christ did when He lived on the earth and died on the cross. The Shepherd of the sheep led by example with the big picture in mind.

chapter five

LOVE IS THE 'O$_2$' IN LIFE

LOVE IS A CONCEPT PEOPLE LIKE TO DAYDREAM ABOUT. LOVE IS A WORD WE use to describe anything we like. "I love that movie." "This is my favorite pizza. I love it." "Math class is my best subject. I love it." (Actually, I don't know anyone who says that last one.)

Love is a common term used to describe ordinary items and feelings, like pets, cars and music, things that aren't really that lovely at all. At least, not if we're going to compare it to the love of God. It has become such a trite word in modern conversation.

In ancient Persia, they used eighty different words for love. The classical Indian language called Sanskrit had ninety-six different words for love. In English, we have but one. I'm certainly not suggesting we change that; I'm suggesting we understand the intended use for that word so that it doesn't become stale. When we don't understand the value of a word, we overuse it. When we value something, we use it very carefully.

The word God uses for love is meant to change humanity, but our common use reduces its power to change us. We do a disservice to ourselves by making godly fabric into everyday clothes. We must remind ourselves daily of the uncommon love God expressed to us through His Son Jesus.

The word of God describes love as this:

And so faith, hope, love abide [faith—conviction and belief respecting man's relation to God and divine things; hope—joyful and confident expectation of eternal salvation; love—true affection for God and man, growing out of God's love for and in us], these three; but the greatest of these is love.

—1 Corinthians 13:13, AMP

One day, a group of us in the city were preaching the gospel on the streets downtown. Often I would pair myself up with someone who had a little less experience so I could encourage them. After carefully observing me minster to some people, I prompted my partner to give it a try. He was so anxious to witness that he yelled from a distance across the parking lot to a gentleman walking by.

"God loves you!" he shouted enthusiastically.

And the young feisty man turned around and said smugly, "Yeah? Well, what if He just really likes me?"

How clever, I thought. My second thought was, how empty can a person be inside? Three important words had been spoken, and they hadn't moved him? God the omnipresent, omnipotent, omniscient creator of heaven and earth loves, embraces, and accepts us as individuals, not for our talents or what we can do for Him and he felt nothing?

Then I recalled my own past, before my encounter with the mighty God I describe. My understanding of love was based on performance and how I made other people feel about themselves. Most of the love and acceptance we've experienced prior to Christ was based on behavior. How we contributed to a job, a team, or a relationship. That love came with conditions based on our ability to provide satisfying results.

Before my encounter with Christ, I would have defined love as an emotional or physical connection—that butterfly feeling. As good as those feelings can be, it's still established on carnality and selfish motives, vulnerable to emotional highs and lows.

Those encounters are often our introduction to love. They are our primary experiences. Because this is our first exposure to love, it seems more real to us. We assume love is something that makes us feel an irregular, excitable emotion.

Have you ever heard someone adamantly say, "I don't want to be married"? Essentially, they're stating that they don't want to have a close intimate connection with an unconditional acceptance. That is the intended premise of the marriage covenant and a natural human desire. Rejecting a natural desire comes from prior disappointing experiences with other imperfect human beings. It becomes easier to suppress that emotion than to process its reality and renew our minds.

With every negative love encounter, our capacity to understand and trust in God's love is reduced. The volume in the heart of mankind has difficulty separating human and divine love. By nature, we restrict the love of God from changing us. Our familiarity dictates truth to us instead of faith.

Everlasting love is much more than an emotional connection; true love is a divine covenant. God's love in the human heart is a miracle.

> ...for God's love has been poured out in our hearts through the Holy Spirit Who has been given to us.
>
> —Romans 5:5, AMP

God has poured everlasting love into our hearts. Every human being has a capacity for the dwelling place of God, a spiritual location woven into our human design. No trespassing is allowed by any demon, confusion, or idol. Until we become born again, this dwelling place remains vacant, set aside by our Creator who desires us to make a free will decision to invite Him in.

When God's love is poured into our hearts, the magnitude of His perfect love can be overwhelming. In an attempt to process His love for us, we compare it to our own experiences with love, and these failures create doubt and misunderstandings about His divine love. The human heart is like a fridge. When we become born again, the fridge turns on and begins to do what it was designed to do. Every negative encounter regarding love is like a fridge magnet to remind us of the experience, so every time we look within our hearts, we first see the failures. The light is on inside, but we see the magnets, and the magnets seem more real to us. We have to go through the magnets on the door to get inside, so we become reluctant to open the fridge to God's love and abundant life.

God wants us to take down all the magnets of the past so that we can have raw, unfiltered access to His divine love provisions. The magnets only distract us from the purpose of the fridge. The purpose of the fridge is not to be a magnet display. It doesn't make any sense to have a two-hundred-pound appliance to present magnets of no value, but that's most often what people see; they never open the fridge. If only they could get beyond the surface where God's love is poured into our hearts.

The purpose of God's love is to display Himself through us. So that we may have the courage to turn from our past experiences and love our neighbors with His divine love, not with our complicated love lives.

> *And we know (understand, recognize, are conscious of, by observation and by experience) and believe (adhere to and put faith in and rely on) the love God cherishes for us. God is love...*
>
> —1 John 4:16, AMP

God is *love!* Love created us! Love formed us and knew us in the womb. Love brought us forth unto the earth. We give our parents credit, but we are missing the Source. Without God, our parents would produce nothing. But God can produce offspring without two parents. Just ask the virgin Mary. Love is the most powerful force on earth!

Because God is love. The Scriptures don't say He *has* love, they say He *is* love. You can try to describe this unfailing love, but in our human limitations we cannot understand its depth.

> *...the Lord delights in those who fear him, who put their hope in his unfailing love.*
>
> —Psalm 147:11, NIV

Human love is like the automobiles we buy; they are designed to break down. But God's love will never fail us. This life is where two love stories collide—our complicated love and the love of Christ. One has an unhappy ending, but the other love story has no ending at all, because it is eternal and unfailing!

> *But the eyes of the Lord are on those who fear him, on those whose hope is in his unfailing love...*
>
> —Psalm 33:18, NIV

Doubt cannot destroy it and our faith cannot create it. It is God's to give and it flows to us through His Son. We can only receive God's love by revelation. When we receive the revelation, we receive the manifestation! We have to receive it by faith, because anything we want to receive in the Kingdom of God must be received by faith first.

We can only love with divine love after we accept it. We know that God loves us, but have we accepted it, or received it, in order to have the knowledge revealed to our inner man?

We may know about His perfect love and not dispute that, but it's more difficult to believe that God, being perfect, could unfailingly love someone like us, who is imperfect. So we keep a safe distance, to protect ourselves because of logical information retained by our past conclusions regarding human love.

God desires us to understand the character of His love opposed to human love. God's love is Jesus Christ Himself manifest in the flesh.

For God so loved the world that He gave his Son among many sons—no!—His only begotten Son so that whomever believes in Him shall not perish but have everlasting life (John 3:16).

> *No one has greater love [no one has shown stronger affection] than to lay down (give up) his own life for his friends.*
>
> —John 15:13, AMP

Love has forgiven our darkest sins. When you sin, do you call yourself names that God has not called you? Loser, failure, bad Christian? Do you punish yourself when you do wrong? Punishment doesn't forgive guilt. Love does!

Old Testament law demanded a blood sacrifice from human hands for sin and the Scriptures say there is a better way.

> *For if that first covenant had been without defect, there would have been no room for another one or an attempt to institute another one.*
> —Hebrews 8:7, AMP

The old covenant was for spiritually dead men. Love replaces the law. Love convicts and the law condemns. Love died for you on the cross and the law sentences us to death. Love appeals to us and the law judges us.

Our remorse over sinful behavior can subtly convince us that we are unworthy of God's love. We have knowledge of God's love for us, but we don't live perpetually in His love because we know our natural tendencies to behave contrary to God's Word. But it is the Holy Spirit that makes us holy, not self-discipline! God loves you in spite of your behavior. We walk by what we believe in His Word, not by what we see in our surroundings.

We cannot love others with His love until we possess and accept this great gift. This needs to be our primary experience of love.

> *God is love, and he who dwells and continues in love dwells and continues in God, and God dwells and continues in him.*
> —1 John 4:16, AMP

To walk in love is to walk with God, and to walk with God is to walk in love. The deeper you know love, the deeper you know God. The platform of God's love is revelation then manifestation, not imagination or previous life experiences. His love is gentle, unfading, and ever ready to believe the best of every person. Surrender yourself to His love so He may have His way.

> *In this is love: not that we loved God, but that He loved us and sent His Son to be the propitiation (the atoning sacrifice) for our sins.*
> —1 John 4:10, AMP

Love is the 'O₂' in Life

Why is love so important?

If I [can] speak in the tongues of men and [even] of angels, but have not love (that reasoning, intentional, spiritual devotion such as is inspired by God's love for and in us), I am only a noisy gong or a clanging cymbal.

And if I have prophetic powers (the gift of interpreting the divine will and purpose), and understand all the secret truths and mysteries and possess all knowledge, and if I have [sufficient] faith so that I can remove mountains, but have not love (God's love in me) I am nothing (a useless nobody).

Even if I dole out all that I have [to the poor in providing] food, and if I surrender my body to be burned or in order that I may glory, but have not love (God's love in me), I gain nothing.

—1 Corinthians 13:1–3, AMP

Love is the centerpiece, the main attraction on earth. All mankind desires and strives for it and God is willing to work all things out through love.

Why is it with our hearts that we love?

No matter your race, age, gender, or religion, if you have the breath of life, you have a heart and you long for love and acceptance. The desires of the heart bind all mankind together. Love is the oxygen of life and is a deep yearning in the genetic make up of mankind.

Our eyes are composed of over two million working parts. When we touch something, we send a message to our brain at 124 miles per hour. Our bodies are made of incomprehensible construction, but God designed everything to work through the heart. If the heart doesn't work, neither do the eyes or sense of touch.

Have you ever noticed that it doesn't feel right to leave a birthday party until the person celebrating her birthday has had some birthday cake? If you tell the host that you have to leave early, their response will be, "You should wait until we present the cake." We can have candles, party hats, gifts, and birthday songs—everything else seems negotiable.

Why? Because the cake is the centerpiece of the party, just as God's love is the centerpiece of who He is.

You can be a powerful prophet, understand all the secret truths, and have faith to move mountains—but if you don't have love, you gain nothing. Love activates and energizes our faith to love others beyond what we are capable of expressing in the natural.

> *For [if we are] in Christ Jesus, neither circumcision nor uncircumcision counts for anything, but only faith activated and energized and expressed and working through love.*
>
> —Galatians 5:6, AMP

Faith works through love, and love flows out through our faith. Our faith will not be effective without love; one needs the other. Faith and love is like peanut butter and jelly, always sticking together.

While on a mission trip in Africa, I was evangelizing a village in Malawi, going from hut to hut, when I approached one house where the residents didn't immediately arise to come and greet me. The incident struck me as strange because of the village's hospitable culture. I came upon a mother who appeared very sick and tired. Her eyes were closed with her tongue protruded slightly from her mouth. She was dying of malaria.

I noticed a lump on the ground with a thin white cloth covering the entire lump.

"What is wrong with this family?" I asked my interpreter.

The mother peeled back the thin cloth and I saw a child under two asleep with flies buzzing around her. She had been old enough to walk, but not old enough to understand what fire can do to the body. She had walked into the campfire and remained standing in it, knowing that it hurt but not knowing what to do to stop the pain. Because of the mother's condition, she hadn't been able to protect the child.

The child's leg was burned so badly that raw flesh was exposed. There was black-charred skin, dry blood, and clear liquid oozing out of the wound. Forgive me for describing it this way, but these were my real-time thoughts; her leg looked like a piece of raw meat that people put on the barbecue.

"My daughter cried until she could not cry anymore," the mother said.

My immediate response was natural. "Let's throw Mom and baby in the car and get her to the hospital right away!"

The interpreter said that there was no car in the village.

"I know a pastor with a car," I said. "I'll get him on the phone."

"If you take this family to the hospital, there will be no supplies there for them," the interpreter insisted.

"Where is the father?" I urgently asked.

The mother responded by saying that the father had not been around for a long time. This family was hopeless and mere hours from death.

The mother had given up, perhaps because of sickness, perhaps because of the guilt of not being able to save her child.

My heart was so broken for this child. She was innocent. I became like a temporary father to this child—not in physical care, but spiritual care. We prayed and I wept like this was my only child. I couldn't speak to God with traditional verbal prayer, because tears took my breath away.

I muttered in my heart to the Lord, "If you really love me, save this child!"

I would never, ever say a prayer like that with my natural mind; it came out before I could process it. I don't have the courage to be so bold as to ask God to prove His love for me. I know He loves me, but in this case it was too late.

The father of the fatherless inserted me into this situation. I loved this child like I had raised her. I felt responsibility for her like I would have gladly traded places with her. That night, I hardly slept because of my weeping prayer for that baby.

The next morning, I took a small team back to the village to check on the child.

I approached the hut to see a woman sitting outside. I asked my interpreter, "Where is the mother of the child?"

"I am her!" the woman interjected.

"No," I said. "You cannot be. The mother of the child was at least fifteen years older than you."

"I woke up this morning, healed by God!"

Overcome with emotion, I was unable to formulate words. But knowing the character of God, I said to myself, "He would never bring a dying mom back to life to let the baby die. That is just not His nature."

We prayed for the family and rejoiced at the mom's supernatural recovery, even though the condition of the baby had not changed.

The following day, as the team and I moved on to preach the gospel to another village, one of our team leaders went back to the village without me knowing, to check on the family. He later said that he hadn't taken me because of how emotionally draining he'd thought it would be for me. He did, however, take a digital camera and took close up pictures of the baby girl.

The pictures were of the leg which, without any real medical attention, had closed up and turned pink and began scarring in less than twenty-four hours.

You can guess my reaction. I was filled with love for a faithful God who had caused His healing power to do exactly what He says it will do.

As you can imagine, we found favor with the villages when testimony spread of the manifest healing and love of God through His children. The amazing part of this story is that the highlight to the villages wasn't the healing power of God as much as it was the love and concern expressed by total strangers for the family. God's love offers you protection that no institution or person can provide.

> ...but the One Who was begotten of God carefully watches over and protects him [Christ's divine presence within him preserves him against the evil], and the wicked one does not lay hold (get a grip) on him or touch [him].
>
> —1 John 5:18, AMP

When satan attacks you, the police can't stop him, alarm systems won't detect him, and insurance companies can't reimburse your losses. The protection you have is the love of God. It insulates you in the loving embrace of Jesus.

> *For I am persuaded beyond doubt (am sure) that neither death nor life,*
> *nor angels nor principalities, nor things impending and threatening nor*
> *things to come, nor powers, nor height nor depth, nor anything else in*
> *all creation will be able to separate us from the love of God which is in*
> *Christ Jesus our Lord.*
>
> —Romans 8:38–39, AMP

We should all aspire to love with God's love. We can only do that because He loved us first, and we must welcome His acceptance of us.

Because of our poor self-image, counting ourselves unworthy, we refuse to accept God's love. We measure our worth in the natural to a standard that was achieved by Jesus in the supernatural. The comparison is like pouring sugar in a gas tank or gasoline in baked goods. We consume both sugar and gasoline, but they are completely different methods of consumption.

None of us are worthy of the heavenly Father's goodness and mercy, but it doesn't change the scripture which says that nothing in all creation can separate us from the love of God.

We're not coming to Him based on our worth. Rather, we're coming to Him based on His grace. Remember that in our daily development, our position as loved children is secure in Christ.

chapter six

GRACE IS MORE

WHEN WE WERE KIDS SITTING AROUND THE TABLE AT THANKSGIVING, somebody would say, "Who's going to say grace?" And I'd pretend like I was an old man taking a nap in my chair, like I hadn't heard correctly. "Grace?" I'd say. "Grace passed away fifteen years ago!"

I would ignorantly joke about grace because I had no comprehension of its unfathomable value.

For some people, that's as far as they are acquainted with grace. It's a way of giving thanks to God prior to a meal. Grace is a common word among us. We say it, we thank God for it, we wish it on others, but we don't always understand its application in our lives.

Consider the legal profession. We all use basic legal terms, and even abide by the law, but many of us don't have an in-depth understanding of how it applies to our lives until we find ourselves in a specific situation.

Or consider a dentist. We all have teeth that we use every day. Most of us even brush them every day. However, we don't have a deeper understanding of how to care for them. The dentist does, and as a result he or she is in an empowered position.

Do you pay your lawyer? Your dentist? These professionals profit because they have pursued a greater understanding of a specific topic that is commonly needed.

But for many of us, we only know about grace in general terms, like we do the law and oral care. We must understand grace and apply the reality of it to our lives routinely to benefit through God's blessing, as was His intention.

If I were to ask for an explanation of the grace of God, many would revert back to their salvation experience. The conventional thought process among Christians is that we are saved by His grace. A common thread that emerges is that grace is a free gift and we are justified by His grace and forgiven of our sins.

All of these are absolutely correct, but does the grace of God stop producing in our lives after salvation? Why are we tempted to limit the grace of God to just being a free gift with a one-time use? Grace is not a get out of jail card in the game of monopoly that relies on the chances of picking that card from the deck again.

Grace is a gift, not a loan. How many gifts do you borrow or give back? Grace is certainly salvation and forgiveness of sin. So when we sin, we can acknowledge the grace of God; we comfort ourselves that we are still forgiven because of His grace in our lives.

Saved by grace! This is powerful, but the power doesn't stop producing there. Because of our understanding, and out of overwhelming gratitude for His immense saving grace we are reluctant to anticipate more value in His gift to us.

One of the strategies of satan is to tranquilize believers' perception of grace, to nullify its power in our everyday lives, as if to say that grace is for salvation, but that is where its advantage ends. The devil is seducing all of humanity to believe that grace is just not enough. He wants us to believe that the power of grace stops at salvation. He can't force us into believing something, but he attempts to persuade us with consistent messages of doubt and deception.

Our lack of understanding makes the grace of God less accessible in our lives, even though it's available. We accept loss and defeat because of our lack of understanding.

I recently converted my propane barbecue to a natural gas barbecue. I wanted to switch over because my propane often runs out and I need to get it refilled. There are limitations to using a propane tank. Meanwhile, I already have an endless supply of natural gas pipelined into my house—more gas than I could ever use for my barbecue.

Here is where we get held up regarding the power of the grace of God.

I have an abundant supply of gas to feed this barbecue, but I lack the conversion coupler called faith to access the abundant supply. Without that converter, though I have an immeasurable supplier (Jehovah Jireh), I still operate on propane because I believe it's my only option. Propane is good. It works, but there is something better. I just need to stir up my faith by acting upon my belief that there's something more in grace than salvation.

God's grace and power is available, but not accessible, when we believe that it's just for salvation or just for forgiveness of sin. Our belief system limits the power of grace in our lives.

I live out in a rural area, and my internet signal used to become intermittent. When I called technical support, they always ran me through the same troubleshooting tests to arrive at the same conclusion. The signal to the tower was strong. The signal from the tower to my modem was strong. So the problem had to be in the link between my modem and my router. Technical support referred to it as "bottlenecking." The power was there, but something was hindering its extensive capabilities.

With this understanding, I purchased a more suitable router that relieved my frustrations and empowered the equipment to work to its full potential and design. God's unmerited grace toward mankind is sometimes bottlenecked because we don't understand its effectiveness. The power is present, but our faith hinders its potency.

> *But He said to me, My grace (My favor and loving-kindness and mercy) is enough for you [sufficient against any danger and enables you to bear the trouble manfully]; for My strength and power are made perfect (fulfilled and completed) and show themselves most effective in [your] weakness. Therefore, I will all the more gladly glory in my weaknesses and infirmities, that the strength and power of Christ (the Messiah) may rest (yes, may pitch a tent over and dwell) upon me!*
>
> —2 Corinthians 12:9, AMP

Who wants to go camping? Who wants the power of God resting over them like a tent?

Grace has more than one operation in our lives. Yes, we are saved by it. It's a free gift. But this is not just a defensive gift of survival, to be called on when we're in really desperate times.

God's strength and power is made perfect and brought into completion (is most effective) in our weakness. When you are strong, His strength is not as effective. Why do we hide from weakness? Avoid weakness? Deny weakness? Our weakness is where the power of God is most evident! I must decrease so that He may increase!

Perhaps you say, "My teacher always put me down," or "I get angry because of my dad," or "No one believes in me so I can never..." or "I'm not qualified to..." There is no one among us who doesn't have those thoughts. We all have moments of doubt where we lack faith.

Paul says that we should boast in our weakness all the more so that God's power can rest upon us like a tent pitched over our lives. Therefore our weakness—where we lack, where we have arrested development, where life hasn't been fair to us—is God's opening to put His strength on full display!

Grace is God's divine ability given as a gift unto man to bring His glory and power to establish His Kingdom here on earth as it is in heaven. God uses us earthlings to produce heavenly principles and benefits for His people through the gift of His grace.

Even Jesus, while on earth, had the grace of God upon His life to achieve what He needed to do.

And the Child grew and became strong in spirit, filled with wisdom; and the grace (favor and spiritual blessing) of God was upon Him.
—Luke 2:40, AMP

The introduction of grace in the Scriptures leaves a lasting impression with its first mention in Genesis:

So the Lord said, I will destroy, blot out, and wipe away mankind, whom I have created from the face of the ground—not only man, [but] the beasts and the creeping things and the birds of the air—for it grieves Me and makes Me regretful that I have made them.

But Noah found grace (favor) in the eyes of the Lord.

—Genesis 6:7–8, AMP

Grace can cause us to be picked out among mankind. It can even extend the blessing to the people around us, as Noah's family found out. The Bible doesn't say that Noah's family found favor, but that Noah did, and his family was extended grace through his life.

Some of us say in our hearts, *There's no way my brother would ever accept Christ. There's no hope for my mother.* What about the divine power operating in our own lives? Grace has a longer reach than we think. There is no place it cannot infuse if it finds an open vessel in the vicinity.

Grace establishes us against all obstacles.

And Joseph was brought down to Egypt; and Potiphar, an officer of Pharaoh, the captain and chief executioner of the [royal] guard, an Egyptian, bought him from the Ishmaelites who had brought him down there. But the Lord was with Joseph, and he [though a slave] was a successful and prosperous man; and he was in the house of his master the Egyptian. And his master saw that the Lord was with him and that the Lord made all that he did to flourish and succeed in his hand.

—Genesis 39:1–3, AMP

And Joseph found grace in his sight, and he served him: and he made him overseer over his house, and all that he had he put into his hand.

—Genesis 39:4, KJV

Grace will take us from being a slave to a governor. Joseph went from serving Potiphar to commanding Potiphar. When Joseph was in the pit, I imagine him saying, *My destiny is not down here! The dream I had was not being thrown into a pit by my brothers, but my brothers bowing to me.* Grace rescued him from the pit where his brothers sought to leave him and established him in a foreign land, where he later saved the lives of those very same brothers. Joseph's brothers left for dead the very person who was to bring them life, because of grace. Even with the brothers' bad decision, in defiance to the dream God gave Joseph, their lives were still preserved.

Grace will move you into position to fulfill what God has predestined you to do. Joseph was too strong around his family. He needed to be moved among the Egyptians for God's grace to be displayed in him so no human system of fortune or favor could lay claim to the glory.

What about Mary the mother of Jesus?

> *And he came to her and said, Hail, O favored one [endued with grace]! The Lord is with you! Blessed (favored of God) are you before all other women!*
>
> —Luke 1:28, AMP

Grace permits you to take on an assignment that no other human in history could take on. Try raising God manifest in the flesh. What parenting book could you read? What advice could Grandma give? This is Jesus the only begotten son of God. The immensity of your assignment doesn't matter; as long as you have access to God's power, it is sufficient.

> *Now Stephen, full of grace (divine blessing and favor) and power (strength and ability) worked great wonders and signs (miracles) among the people.*
>
> —Acts 6:8, AMP

Grace endorses you, and you will be a representative of His product! Many famous people attach their names to products in exchange for financial reward. God's grace attaches His reputation to us and our endeavours.

Stephen was full of grace and operated in the divine power of God to showcase what the Lord can accomplish through mankind. God stands by His product and His endorsement.

When somebody endorses you, that person speaks highly of you. They are the references on your resume. If your potential employer contacts your references, you can be confident that they will endorse you. They will sing your praises because they only see the good in you!

With a powerful endorsement, your employer doesn't have to dig deep into your past to check on your background.

And with great strength and ability and power the apostles delivered their testimony to the resurrection of the Lord Jesus, and great grace (loving-kindness and favor and goodwill) rested richly upon them all.
—Acts 4:33, AMP

Grace also provides authorization. We sign paperwork at the bank because the tellers need permission to move our money around. The grace of God causes us to operate in boldness, like we own the place. Grace is His consent to the usage of His power.

Many condo buildings are secured electronically, so you need to have a key fob to enter the building. The grace of God is like the electronic security system in the spirit because it opens doors that no one shall shut, and shuts doors that no one shall open (Revelation 3:7).

Have you ever approached a person attempting to get into a secure building without their key? They get frustrated, desperate, and impatient. Have you ever had the pleasure to be the savior who appears at the door with the key fob in your hand? You're so willing to accommodate because it feels good to help out somebody who's in a jam, because we've all been in that position. The key fob of faith accesses that electronic door of grace. God is pleased to open doors that seem impossible to open because in that event, it displays that power belongs to God.

Grace is the power of the Holy Spirit operating in our routine daily activities to exhibit the transfer of divine empowerment to open human vessels.

In high school, I failed Grade Ten math. In fact, my math teacher said there was no way *in heaven* I would even graduate high school. He classified me as a careless student who would never understand the concepts. The worst part is that I believed him, because nobody told me anything different.

I did go to university, but I always avoided the pure math classes, believing they weren't meant for me to touch. I was fine with that, as long as I didn't have to confront the dreaded M-word: mathematics.

Nonetheless, I eventually became a schoolteacher. After my first full year of teaching and a double major in kinesiology and social science (everything but math), my administrator approached me to explain that my probationary position would end the next year, but she wanted to keep me around as a... don't say the M-word... mathematics teacher.

So I did what anybody would do to keep a job they loved. "Yea! Math? No problems there! I can teach math!"

In my math class, I had a teacher's aide to assist my students with special needs. She just happened to breathe mathematics. All her training and education majors were in math. It is one challenge to convince students that you know what you're talking about, and quite another to convince a math major. This aide was always present during my lessons, and one day she approached me to debrief regarding the lesson.

My natural thought: *Oh boy, what did I do wrong?* Instead she said something that changed my life: "You have a quick and strong math mind." I looked behind me to see who she was talking to!

It turned out that I wasn't so bad at math after all, because in my second full year my school made me the lead math teacher. As a reminder of what the grace of God can do, former students still approach me to say things like, "If it wasn't for you in math class, I wouldn't have stood a chance."

Such a reward is better than any paycheque. Math was a failed topic from my past, and I would have preferred to avoid it and hide in a closet, but God wanted me to face this mountain head on just to show me what I, empowered by the grace of God, was capable of.

If the generations of my family had remained on course, I would have inherited the name Jason Torgusen. The name Torger is a variant of Old Norse given to the God of Thunder, also referred to as Thor, whose name is associated with war. So you could say I was due to inherit the name "son of war."

My great-grandfather murdered my great-grandmother and then committed suicide, leaving behind their one-year-old boy, whom I grew up calling Grandpa. He was adopted by a family with the surname Johnson. Johnson means "son of John." The name John translates to grace or favor. Therefore, I went from being a son of thunder and war to a son of His grace! My name is favor! A precious picture of salvation is displayed in my bloodline.

Hopelessness from the pit of darkness tried to end my family on earth, but Jehovah adopted us as orphans and put His seal and name upon us!

Paul says,

> *Grace and peace be yours in abundance through the knowledge of God and of Jesus our Lord. His divine power has given us everything we need for a godly life through our knowledge of him who called us by his own glory and goodness.*
>
> —2 Peter 1:2-3, NIV

So how do we receive this infinite grace? That's just it. We have already received it; we just access it by faith in our daily walk.

We are saved by grace... through faith! Grace and faith got us this far, so why stop there?

chapter seven

RIGHTEOUSNESS IS JUST RIGHT

"WHY DOES MY CAR MAKE THAT STRANGE SOUND?" YOU ASK THE MECHANIC. You're not aware that the fuel pump is causing it to sputter, so you tolerate it. It doesn't stop you from driving it, because the car still functions. The sound causes uncertainty, is annoying, and makes you vulnerable due to lack of understanding. If it's left unchecked long enough, it will cause you to park the car permanently.

Sometimes we have access to understanding but never pursue it properly because we don't comprehend the value. I've collected Air Miles since 1997 and I've never bothered to go through the process to put them to use. I own them, but can't be motivated to sort out the procedure, until recently I got a letter saying that the rules have changed and now my Air Miles will be expiring.

Before I ever used even one benefit, they're going to begin reducing my Air Miles. I suffer loss because I cannot be troubled to gain comprehension of the program.

An imperative foundation to apply to our daily walk is the understanding of the righteousness of God.

Righteousness is His nature. It is an essential quality that demonstrates His being.

In His days Judah shall be saved and Israel shall dwell safely: and this is His name by which He shall be called: The Lord Our Righteousness.

—Jeremiah 23:6, AMP (emphasis added)

Not the Lord God *is* righteous, but that righteousness is who He is. Righteousness is an everyday word in our terminology, so we need to be reminded of the undiluted value of His righteousness.

Righteousness and justice are the foundation of Your throne; mercy and loving-kindness and truth go before Your face.

—Psalm 89:14, AMP

It is the essence of God to be just and righteous. It is in His fabric. It is natural to Him. There is no injustice in Him.

Was it not I, the Lord? And there is no other God besides Me, a rigidly and uncompromisingly just and righteous God and Savior; there is none besides Me.

—Isaiah 45:21, AMP

I used to work down in the bayou around New Orleans. While there, a friend of mine decided that he was going to catch an alligator and take it home to his children for a pet. As if the thought wasn't silly enough...

Well, he caught a young four-footer and had to duct tape its mouth shut to bring him back to the hotel. Seems ridiculous, doesn't it? Why? Because it's in the nature of the alligator to bite people. You cannot change the nature of the alligator; you remove that duct tape and he is going to bite, no matter how friendly we are. It's in his genetic makeup.

If a butterfly lands on your arm, most people would hold still and take in the moment, almost afraid to breathe so they could get a closer look. Why? Because it's in the nature of that insect to be beautiful and captivating.

Now, when a mosquito lands on your arm you can't kill that un-tamed wild beast fast enough—because we know it's in its nature to bite people!

It is God's nature to be righteous, not a separate act. In fact, we can't define God by righteousness as much as we can define righteousness by God. Would we ever define water by fish? We cannot define fish without water because fish apart from water would cease to exist. Fish need the water, but the water doesn't need the fish.

We need God first to be the righteousness of God. Righteousness is right standing of man before God.

In the beginning of the Bible, Genesis demonstrates this theme.

And the man and his wife were both naked and were not embarrassed or ashamed in each other's presence.

—Genesis 2:25, AMP

That is the state of righteousness: completely free, unashamed, and in close communion with the Lord.

The very next chapter describes the story of this same man, his wife, and the subtle, crafty creature. Satan uses the oldest trick in the book, making us believe that we need something more than what we have. He entices our human craving through a consistent message of rebellion.

Can it really be? Satan asked the woman a question to plant a seed of doubt. Then he appealed to her mind of reasoning by saying that she would not die. Satan continued to speak deceitfully for God by saying that He knows Eve will become like Him, to know the difference between good and evil.

After Adam and Eve bit into the forbidden fruit,

the eyes of them [Adam and Eve] both were opened, and they knew that they were naked

—Genesis 3:7, AMP

They became self-aware of their disobedience. They recognized that they were no longer in right standing with God because of their sin.

Prior to this, Adam and God seemed to have a great relationship. God gave him a garden to work in, let him name all the creatures, and even created a woman to bless him.

When Adam and Eve ate of the fruit and sin entered mankind, it was accredited to us that we would be born into a sin nature. Because of this event, it is in the unregenerate man's nature to sin.

Adam and Eve had been naked and unashamed. As soon as sin awareness entered mankind, Adam and Eve tried to mask their nakedness with fig leaves. Though their physical condition hadn't changed, they tried to cover up their nakedness. They tried to manage their sin by presenting a different image than their shame. Have we not all tried to do the same to deal with our conscience?

Then God called to Adam, "Where are you?"

Adam responded, "I was afraid because I was naked, so I hid myself."

This is the state of a sinner hiding his condition from God because his remorse for disobedience causes him to feel unworthy in His presence. Yet God knew exactly where Adam was, just as He is aware of what state we are all in regardless of our personal confession or public appearance. Adam's reaction to God shows us that a negative self-image, fear, and unworthiness are all signs of a guilty conscience.

Of course Adam blamed the woman. And then the woman blamed the serpent. The serpent didn't take responsibility, because even it knew that God was omniscient. Guilt causes us to justify our actions; it is our internal need for redemption.

When we're in right standing with God, we have no need to be deceptive, avoid responsibility, and fear man. Righteousness lets us know who we are in Christ, and it has nothing to do with our own accomplishments or good behavior.

Adam was created to have life. In a sense, we could say he was born to life. From birth, he was together with God in constant fellowship. When sin entered man, Adam went from life to death, from together with God to separate from God.

If you take a living organism and separate it from its origin, it begins to die. There is a plant in my backyard that has been removed from the dirt. The leaves have turned brown and shrivelled up. There are no signs of life anymore. Because of our sin nature, we have become separated from our Creator. We could say that we are born into death. We are born into a sin nature, so we have to go from death to life, from separated to together with God.

Adam went from a divine and blameless conscience to a guilty conscience. We must go from a guilty conscience to a divine and blameless conscience.

Christ restored access to the state of righteousness (right standing with God) that Adam and Eve lost in the garden. We forfeited that relationship because of deception and lust. Unrighteousness is a sense of unworthiness which comes from the awareness of our guilt because of the fall.

Jesus had our backs and an answer to the separation from God issue when He died on the cross. Sin doesn't disconnect those who have come to believe in Christ from God anymore. God raised us up with Christ and seated us with Him in heavenly places.

Every major religion is aware that there is something broken in mankind. What separates the followers of Christ is that His death made atonement to remit our sin and guilt. We accept the gospel of Jesus Christ as truth, the free gift of salvation, grace, and that righteousness is bestowed upon us—not at the work or expense of mankind, but at the cost of God's only begotten Son, Jesus.

No other major world religion seems to offer righteousness and grace. They all require some type of works. Jesus Christ is also the only religious figure to say that He was God manifest in the flesh, and He verified this statement by resurrecting after three days. He then showed Himself to five hundred witnesses to confirm God's express power.

For if because of one man's trespass (lapse, offense) death reigned through that one, much more surely will those who receive [God's] overflowing grace (unmerited favor) and the free gift of righteousness [putting them into right standing with Himself] reign as kings in life through the one Man Jesus Christ (the Messiah, the Anointed One).

—Romans 5:17, AMP

If it were left up to Adam, we would all be dead men in our sin. But Jesus came to represent mankind and brought us life through His obedience, inaugurating our righteousness.

> *For just as by one man's disobedience (failing to hear, heedlessness, and carelessness) the many were constituted sinners, so by one Man's obedience the many will be constituted righteous (made acceptable to God, brought into right standing with Him).*
>
> —Romans 5:19, AMP

Were we there at the fall of mankind? No, but sin still entered mankind and we didn't do anything to encourage it. But the Scriptures say that through one Man's obedience, righteousness with God was made available to us all.

We inherited sin by our indirect actions, but once we receive grace or become born of the spirit we receive righteousness, also by our indirect actions. We were not present at the crucifixion either. Adam got us into this disarray and Jesus got us out! Righteousness restores our fellowship with God by dealing with our inequities once and for all.

In Luke 15, Jesus told the story of the prodigal son. The younger of two sons asked his father prematurely for his inheritance and left his father's house to squander his estate by reckless and loose living. The young man then came to himself and recognized his error and decided to return home. Upon the son's return, his first words were:

> *Father, I have sinned against heaven and in your sight; I am no longer worthy to be called your son [I no longer deserve to be recognized as a son of yours]!*
>
> —Luke 15:21, AMP

He is primarily more conscious of his sin than he is of his customary benefits as a son. It is in his nature to sin, so he finds those attributes easier to relate to and acknowledge, rather than his right to be called a son. Because of the guilt of his sin, he feels unworthy to be called a son or be in right standing with his father!

Guilt causes feelings of unworthiness, making us gullible to satan's lies. When we relate to sin easier than entitlement, we feel remorse, and because of that remorse we attempt to compensate for our behavior.

A person whose conscience prevails towards sin may get a letter from the government tax agency and assume they're being accused of cheating on their taxes. That sense of guilt will make the unopened letter feel like poison ivy in their hands. They could hear a loud knock at the door and in that moment jump from their chair, thinking that the police have surrounded the house. A guilty conscience will cause them to look out the windows for government helicopters dispatched to apprehend them.

But a righteous-thinking man will get the same letter and expect it is regarding a refund to his account, because he knows he is blameless. The righteous person expects favor because he knows who he is, and how he became that way.

When a driver comes across a police check-stop during the holidays, a guilty man will be nervous, remembering all the drinks he's had in the last two years, or recall the parking ticket he hasn't paid yet, though he's been meaning to. The officer asks him, "Have you had anything to drink?" In distress, the driver answers, "Yes, officer. I drank four cups of coffee today, two more than usual!"

But when you know you have nothing to hide, a check-stop is exciting. Because you know it's impossible to be found guilty! You know you are entirely innocent.

That's the way we are supposed to live! There is no condemnation in Christ because of His righteousness imputed unto us! Who are we and to whom do we belong? Sons and daughters, to the Father.

> *But the father said to his bond servants, Bring quickly the best robe (the festive robe of honor) and put it on him; and give him a ring for his hand and sandals for his feet.*
>
> —Luke 15:22, AMP

The father didn't even acknowledge what the son said when he professed his unworthiness. Likewise, our heavenly Father doesn't acknowledge our guilt when we come to Him. He's already moved beyond that, because Jesus was our substitute for the penalty of sin. It is we who feel like the sin hasn't been dealt with.

As far as the east is from the west, so far has He removed our transgressions from us.

—Psalm 103:12, AMP

Instead the Father places the robe, which represents righteousness, on the son. The robe covers his nakedness and indecencies.

I will greatly rejoice in the Lord, my soul will exult in my God; for He has clothed me with the garments of salvation, He has covered me with the robe of righteousness, as a bridegroom decks himself with a garland, and as a bride adorns herself with her jewels.

—Isaiah 61:10, AMP

The robe represents the relationship we have with one another. A company or team jacket tells everyone that we belong to a greater organization, and they have also accepted us for who we are. There is an agreed upon relationship represented through the jacket.

Righteousness gives you a sense of divine entitlement. The robe of righteousness declares to all principalities that you are in right standing with God. That you belong to Him and He has accepted you. Righteousness brings us home. It restores our fellowship with the Father.

Nobody else can speak for the Father except the sons and daughters who manage His estate.

On the farm growing up, random people would stop by to ask my father if they could hunt deer on our land. Now, if my father wasn't home, they would ask me or one of my brothers for permission. Why? In a spiritual sense, I wore the robe and ring of my father. I carried his authority. Asking me was like asking my father. The people asking also understood that I walked in my father's protection. If my answer was no, it wasn't really a no from me—I was just a boy—but it was a no from my father. If my answer was yes, it was my father saying yes.

In order to receive the benefits of God's righteousness, we've got to see ourselves as members of the same family, in the likeness or nature of the Father of that family.

Have you ever heard the expression "She looks just like her father"? If righteousness is God's nature, we resemble that expression, and we're made righteous through Jesus Christ. The natural man begins with a sin nature, but the new creation begins with a righteous nature.

But it is from Him that you have your life in Christ Jesus, Whom God made our Wisdom from God, [revealed to us a knowledge of the divine plan of salvation previously hidden, manifesting itself as] our Righteousness [thus making us upright and putting us in right standing with God], and our Consecration [making us pure and holy], and our Redemption [providing our ransom from eternal penalty for sin].

—1 Corinthians 1:30, AMP

The scripture uses the word *made*, in the past tense. There is nothing left to be done to complete the project. All actions required for these gifts have been concluded by God. We're not talking about a work in progress for these subjects of godly wisdom, righteousness, consecration, and redemption.

The devil has two major schemes to paralyze the benefit of righteousness in light of God's Word. We can find them in Revelation 12: deception through seduction and accusation.

1 Corinthians 15:34 of the King James says, *"Awake to righteousness, and sin not"* (KJV).

Deception tells us that we can't be righteous until we live our lives without sin, but that goes against the truth of God's Word. Satan wants us to understand it backwards. We need to awake to righteousness and sin not, but the doctrine of the devil says, "Sin not and you will have righteousness."

We became righteous not by doing right... right? Romans 5:17 says that when we received grace, we also received God's free gift of righteousness. So why do we now measure righteousness by what we're doing right? Satan wants us to believe that we're righteous until we fail, or that we can sin away God's righteousness in us.

When we walk in righteousness, everything must bow to that imperial relationship with the Father, but the devil is going to accuse us and remind us of our past as sons and daughters of God's wrath. That's who we *were*—and the devil will remind us by bringing to our attention past sins we committed. He'll try to cause us to feel guilty again. He is the accuser. Just because we're free from guilt one day doesn't mean satan will stop accusing. Remember Adam immediately had fear, shame, and a negative self-image because of his guilty conscience.

Have you ever heard a voice say, "You're not a very good Christian"? Accusation! Hear it enough and you'll question yourself. A consistent message is not always a true one.

My wife Andrea tells a story of a girl she went to school with who would say, "That's not very Christian-worthy of you." Of course this was announced in the moments when the girl was recognizing the guilty action of others breaking the standard of God.

Is it possible that our guilt for the sin we still carry somehow gives the devil access to remind us that we'll never be good Christians because of our past sin? When we're still dealing with the guilt and shame of those sins, the accuser brings them to our memory, causing us to feel unworthy of a righteous relationship with God, thereby disabling our authority and protection.

Satan would have us believe we could become righteous by not sinning. To be in right standing with God, we must not fail in obedience. Even as I write that statement, I hear a robotic voice saying it. That pattern of thinking is no different than the Pharisees. We call it self-righteous. They had their own righteousness according to the law.

I bear them witness that they have a [certain] zeal and enthusiasm for God, but it is not enlightened and according to [correct and vital] knowledge. For being ignorant of the righteousness that God ascribes [which makes one acceptable to Him in word, thought, and deed] and

seeking to establish a righteousness (a means of salvation) of their own,
they did not obey or submit themselves to God's righteousness.

—Romans 10:2–3, AMP

The Jews believe that righteousness is received by fulfilling the law, but 1 Timothy 1:9 says that the law is not made for the righteous, that it is made for the lawless.

Legalism tells us that we must have no sin in our lives, that only then can we become righteous! My thought is, how long is that timeframe? As long as the memory of our last sin? And are we depending on the sharpness of human memory to earn our righteousness? That scheme doesn't make logical sense to me.

Righteousness is not a feeling; we walk in its authority by faith. God has to be validated through the senses for those who don't trust entirely in their Father.

Jesus said to Thomas, "You have seen and believed and that is good, but blessed (which in Greek means positioned for God's favor) are those who have not seen and yet have believed" (John 20:29, paraphrased).

We receive righteousness by faith. We're wearing either the robe or fig leaves to cover our nakedness. Why would we work so hard for something we have already received? The sheriff has deputized us, so we just need to walk around with that shiny badge of authority.

In counselling sessions, I hear a common theme among people. It goes something like this: "Well, I've got this part of my life all straightened out and I have victory over here, but there's this one annoying and repetitive sin I struggle with." Struggle with? God has dealt with it. That's just it. It's us struggling instead of turning our entire trust over to God. We trust too much in our own ability. We represent ourselves when we have the best lawyer, who's also the judge willing to represent us. In fact, He has already passed sentence and provided retribution.

Awake to righteousness and sin no more. Be open to the awakening of the revealed Word of God so that the power of the Word may be made plain in your life!

Only Ever

[After all] the kingdom of God is not a matter of [getting the] food and drink [one likes], but instead it is righteousness (that state which makes a person acceptable to God) and [heart] peace and joy in the Holy Spirit.

—Romans 14:17, AMP

Christ's perfect righteousness is applied to imperfect humans that are reminded constantly of that deficit. We combat these accusations daily, hourly if need be, to remind ourselves that His righteousness is just and right for us.

chapter eight

WRONG GUY, RIGHT PLACE, ONLY GOD

GOD CARVED ME OUT AS HIS MINISTER OUTSIDE THE CONVENTIONAL CHURCH walls, apart from Sunday morning services. I became acquainted with the Holy Spirit's voice and conformed to His direction by putting myself into the unknown. I have genuinely needed Him in those moments when I felt unsure what to do next. I surrendered myself to be available to the Holy Spirit for whatever He assigned me to do. I was engaged, willing, and intentional.

My first time ministering a deliverance prayer was with prostitutes hanging outside a strip club late at night looking for work. Feeling the fire burn in my heart, I would go wandering downtown believing God to bring a message of hope through me to the hopeless.

We confronted johns who were there to pick up girls. I would tell the girls that the presence of God was here, and this always seemed to stir up activity. Sometimes I was very unwelcome, and other times girls would break under the gentle pressure of the Holy Spirit, throw away their cigarette, weep, and ask for prayer.

I often heard that I was the first person in a long time who didn't want something from them; I only wanted to show care for them without condition. The Spirit of God would show up and minister directly to His people. At times I put myself in volatile situations in the hope of seeing the captives released. Those times I was in desperate need of the Holy Spirit to come through.

I witnessed my first healing miracle praying for the homeless in a simple outreach program we started by cooking up a roast beef and preparing seventy to a hundred lunches every Saturday. We would take bagged lunches and hot chocolate to give them out near the drug dealers' corners. At times we were threatened verbally, even with baseball bats, and had the police called on us on more than one occasion. Though we were not aggressive. We remained in peace, but the spiritual atmosphere was agitated by our presence.

We would pray for people with their eyes rolled in the back of their heads. We prayed for the self-proclaimed crack addicts in the most dangerous part of town. I felt like these people were closest to dying because of their high-risk lifestyle; therefore they had the shortest amount of time to live and needed the message of salvation urgently.

Our house was like a mini Salvation Army. I parked my cars outside so we could fill our garage with donated clothes for the people in need. Strangers would drive by these areas while we were ministering and donate blankets, Bibles, jackets, steel toe boots, socks, underwear, and even money. We had no ministry name. We never advertised in the church bulletin. Nobody ordained and released us other than the Word of God empowering us. We would simply testify what God was doing in our midst and servants joined our ranks.

I prophesied my first words of wisdom during a cold street evangelism campaign. The knowledge skipped my brain and came right out my mouth without me being able to give it evaluation. I met a girl and knew her name, where she worked, and the condition of her heart before she said a word to me. I shared this with her, and we both stood there with our mouths open, not comprehending what had just happened. I told her it was only God; I wasn't creeping. The presence of God was there. She agreed it could only be Him.

I witnessed my first full room of people to surrender themselves to God inside a maximum security prison where everyone was experiencing the manifest presence of God! This was a room full of tough guys in tears, unashamed to confess their need for a Savior. Jesus was there, and that is all we could say. Hard hearts softened in an institution where showing weakness meant putting your life in danger.

I challenged publicly the doctrine of demons at a local business that was profiting off of selling witchcraft. I stood face to face with four witchdoctors, seeing obvious signs of intense demonic manifestation. The business was only a few blocks from the church and I didn't like praying for the neighborhood with such a blatant advertisement of the enemy close by. Customers walked into the store, saw what was going on, and immediately turned around and left, yet the owner couldn't convince the police to come. On exiting, I proclaimed that if our God was real, this place would not remain. Only four weeks later, I drove by and saw a for sale sign on the building.

The first time I water-baptized someone was in a bathtub at their house after a Bible study. The first message I preached was to my roommates. Three weeks later, two had moved out and the other came to church. The message was love, not condemnation.

I once was preaching the gospel in a village in the interior of Burundi. We needed a signed permit by the governor to go there because we were white people who could become a target for rebels. This hardened village is where people ended up after being displaced by years of civil war. Yet there was no house of God, despite several attempts to establish a church. Residents were hurt, angry, rejected, and outcast.

People were curious, because we were quite obviously visitors. Our team started praying for people who were getting healed in the street. I began preaching a salvation message in the middle of the town. More and more people gathered to see the *mzungu* (white man) shouting outside in the streets. As I continued to share the message of Christ, I made an altar call for all those who wanted to receive Christ and... nothing. I dismissed it, guessing that I'd missed the timing somehow. But I continued pouring my heart out on the streets as more people gathered. I made a second call to salvation, imploring these people that the love of God had accepted them if they would turn from their ways and give their lives to Jesus and... nothing! I knew Christ wanted to save people in this village so I persisted.

What I didn't know is that the ministry team with me had seated all the children behind me. As more people arrived, I called upon the name of the Lord a third time, saying, "There is salvation in and through no one else, for there is no other name under heaven given among men in which we must be saved!"

In my peripheral vision, I saw a hand go up to receive Christ. As I turned to acknowledge that hand, I witnessed all the children behind me raising their hands wanting to receive Christ. Tears rolled down as I turned back to the crowd that had gathered and said, "I tell you the truth, anyone who will not receive the Kingdom of God like these little children will never enter it!"

Suddenly hands began to arise everywhere. The spirit of God began to touch people, and that day a church was planted with eighty members who signed their names to commit to the work.

God used simple children to deliver His message into the hearts of man—not my eloquent or passionate preaching. I was the wrong guy in the right place, at the right time, with the only God.

Action has no season. Acting upon His Word causes things to happen, and intending to act upon the Word causes nothing to happen. Desires are expressed in our speech, but expectations are displayed through our behavior.

God's Word inspired and empowered me. To me it was the "great permission." I didn't wait for my rotation for the Sunday morning pulpit by convincing the senior pastor that I deserved a turn to show that I had been called to minister.

My point is that God didn't need to trust me because of my experience, my knowledge of the Word, my theology degrees, my financial offerings of support, or my lifestyle. He didn't publicly ordain me to take on any of this work. I never thought to develop a team to support the work. He didn't need to trust me, because He was directing me, not the other way around.

I made my Father's business a priority. I made myself available. I was intentional in looking for opportunities. I was willing to follow through with vague plans.

He didn't speak to me directly in a vision or a dream. He didn't even allude to me personally that I would mature as a Christian or that I would treasure those experiences. He made no direct promise that I would be safe or satisfied with the outcome.

My relationship with God emboldened me to realize what I could do for God. I discovered His thoughts towards people. I began to share in the likeness of His heart through prayer, worship, and servanthood.

God doesn't have to come and tell me what I must do for Him. I am in relationship with Him; we are in intimate communication. I hear His call and understand what He wants me to do, and I do it out of a passion to express my love to Him.

My wife doesn't have to ask me to rub her back. I know when she would enjoy a rub because I understand her. I know what pleases her because of close time spent together. God's will is in His Word and the details of His heart are in the time fostered in a close relationship.

We don't have to wait for a voice to come from heaven to say, this is my son in whom I am well pleased. Soul by soul, inch by inch, we take ground for the Lord despite our human behavior. We do our best with what God has put in our hand.

Being available to serve is more powerful than striving for perfection, and it's the greatest threat to satan and his kingdom of darkness. Perfection in people is a false perception. Availability is the main qualifier for engaging in special ops for God. Our weaknesses are made perfect by His power. We all fall short of the glory of God, but we can make ourselves available to be the point of contact for the Almighty in all situations.

Are we available to go where God calls us? To do what He wants us to do? Most answer yes until the question is posed with detail and we're told to go.

What are we doing here and now? What communicates to God that we're available? Do we wait for the perfect scenario, always relying on the next big move of God to inspire us into serving the Lord?

People who hear God's call are those who are serving Him where they are right now. God doesn't waste anything, including our time.

Also I heard the voice of the Lord, saying, Whom shall I send? And who will go for Us?

—Isaiah 6:8, AMP

Who's available? If the grace of God empowers you, what qualifications do you really need? Are you free or do you have "other plans"? The question isn't whether our ability will accomplish the mission; we already know the answer, and it's an emphatic no!

Isaiah 6:8 then adds, *"Here am I; send me!"* It is the cry of every genuine believer who longs to serve God. So why does it seem like church leaders have to beg for volunteers? It's because they have to compete with other life activities. Are Kingdom matters on our priority lists? Do we fit His priorities into our to-do lists? Life becomes out of order if not reevaluated often. Day to day activities will creep up the list unless we're vigilant in guarding our time for a greater purpose.

Jesus said, *"Come after Me [as disciples—letting Me by your Guide], follow Me, and I will make you fishers of men"* (Matthew 4:19, AMP). The next verse says that the disciples at once left their nets and followed Him.

Wait a second. Didn't these guys have jobs? Where were their families? Their wives aren't going to like this! How would they provide for their families? Where would their children go to school? What guarantee did they have from this Messiah? Were there good benefits? They might have been fishermen, but fishers of men? They had no experience in that field. They weren't qualified. They didn't have the education or the resources. They didn't even know what it meant to be a fisher of men. All reasonable questions and thoughts, and all answered by trust in the One who gave the invitation.

Availability makes us vulnerable, but it also makes us powerful. It reminds us that we're not the most important person in the world. Life is not all self-seeking pleasure, selfish ambitions, and self-indulgence. Being available requires making sacrifices, thinking about oneself a little less than before. Being available allows God to display His wonders through us for the sake of His glory. The very events we long to see God do can happen in those moments when we intentionally leave our schedules open and dedicate ourselves to times of worship and servanthood unto the Lord.

And Elijah said to Ahab, Go up, eat and drink, for there is the sound of abundance of rain.

—1 Kings 18:41, AMP

"The sound of the abundance of rain" refers to the sound of the Spirit. If it had been actual rain, they all would have heard it. Elijah had a promise from God, so he went to the top of the mountain to draw close to God and prostrated himself in a position of prayer, which required total surrender. Elijah likely had several items on his mind, but instead he made himself available to see God move in a supernatural way.

Elijah sent his servant seven times to go look for evidence that God was going to move, as if to say, "I'm ready when You are, Lord." He didn't move from that position until the first sign of a cloud, as small as a man's hand, arose out of the sea. Elijah acted quickly by the hand of the Lord that had come upon him. Elijah ran ahead of Ahab's horse. This was a king's horse, presumably the fastest horse around. Elijah ran twenty miles. If Elijah hadn't emptied his schedule and taken his position of surrender and started heading back to Jezreel after receiving the promise of rain, he likely would not have beaten Ahab there. 1 Kings 18:45 says, *"In a little while, the heavens were black with wind-swept clouds..."* (AMP) God postponed the promise of rain until His servant could move into the desired location, at supernatural speed, to show the glory of God. Elijah resisted practical thoughts and made himself accessible to the Spirit to display the wonder of God who hears the prayers of His people.

God conducts His orchestra, but the players have to be paying attention to create beautiful music.

God is able and He is never late. Being available means making time to wait for the promises to come. Don't believe the lie that we're not making a difference. Clearing your agenda to serve God's purpose is a potent ingredient you can add to His recipe, even when the purpose is unknown to you.

chapter nine

FINISH TO THE END

*[Jesus said to God,] I have glorified You down here on the earth by
completing the work that You gave Me to do.*

—John 17:4, AMP

ONE OF THE FIRST MAJOR TESTS OF MY WILL AFTER I COMMITTED MY LIFE
to serve Christ was where I would be located. The city in which God
designated me to do a work was not one I had originally planned to
stay around in. During my daily relationship with the Lord, He asked
me to remain in the local church He had introduced Himself in and
help build the vision. My initial thought was it likely would be for two
years maximum. During that first two years I had asked God in return
that when the time comes for me to go, I don't want to hear it from a
prophet, I don't want circumstances to move me, I don't even want to
feel an unction. I want to hear it directly from You, as clear as the voice
that I heard down in California that brought me here, is as clear as the
voice I want to hear to send me from this place.

Thirteen years later, building the vision of the church, being
tempted to leave for different reasons both good and bad, I engaged
wholeheartedly until my assignment was complete. God honored my
request and spoke clearly to me. Even though I did not expect to remain as long as I did, I am very proud of the way my family and I conducted ourselves in our daily journey. For that reason, when the time

came for us to take a step of faith into the unknown we were confident in God's direction. We left that which we did well.

There is a reward for finishing something. When we graduate from high school or post-secondary, it's not receiving the degree, or even the content of the course that offers the most value. Simple completion of the task brings confidence. There is a reward to all mankind for concluding a work. We gain emotional and mental strength in ourselves. We often hear people say, "It feels so good to finally finish this." They are receiving a blessing from the Lord, whether they're a believer or unbeliever. Rain has no borders, and neither does the blessing of God.

No matter how small a task seems to us, it may not be small to God.

In mathematics, bypassing even a small step can radically change the outcome. We are not aware of every intricate step of the plan God has created for us to walk through, but nothing is wasted. God is efficient.

Some of Christ's last words here on earth, words that echo in our ears, were *"It is finished"* (John 19:30, AMP). Those words were spoken from a beaten body, tired mind, and thirsty mouth. He said this before ascending into glory to be seated at the right hand of the Father. Jesus didn't say "I am finished," even though He was about to die; He said "It is finished." In other words, "My assignment here on earth has concluded, but my actions will live on and continue to deliver millions from the pit of hell."

Jesus followed His mission on earth into death. Nothing could stop Him from bringing to completion heaven's assignment.

It is important to finish what we began so there can be no fractional work to hang over our heads. The accuser loves to remind us that something unfinished is as good as something failed!

Most of the time, our inclination is to think that somebody else will probably finish for us. "I don't think I really have the time. If I had the money, this is what I would do. Somebody else has already done something similar." We prepare to quit rather than prepare to finish. Doubt comes into our thoughts before the process, during the process, and seems to increase near the end of the process.

We excuse ourselves out of work for the Lord, but from the other side of our mouths we cry out for God to employ us to do a great work for Him.

It is our nature, but not our renewed nature, to remain in complacency.

Those initial thoughts after we feel the unction to serve God represent our inner voice trying to delay our instant obedience. Carnality always causes us to second-guess what the Lord has said. We ask ourselves, "Did God really say that?" Sound familiar? If not, look at the story of Eve in Genesis. It's the oldest trick in the book.

Withdrawal should serve as an alarm bell that something isn't right. Somebody else other than God is influencing us to disengage. Our nature is to give God the minimum but expect the maximum return, to be casual with God because it is convenient. Many people find employment and do just enough to not get fired, and in turn employers pay just enough for their workers to not quit.

The sacrifice of comfort, idle time, money, and reputation is difficult but worth it all for the cause of fuelling your passion, that can only be satisfied by your willing partnership for the Lord.

God gave us His sinless Son, His prize to redeem all mankind, yet not all mankind will rest in heaven with Him and some believers are fine with that. We shouldn't be okay with that as believers. We can never give up!

Nehemiah refrained from mingling with pagan gods. He didn't compromise or settle for mediocrity. Nehemiah didn't allow himself time to be idle. He didn't flirt with the practice of paganism. Purpose demanded separation. Nehemiah says, *"Thus I cleansed them [Israelites] from everything foreign"* (Nehemiah 13:30, AMP).

We become easily distracted, finding pleasure in idle pursuits. Satan is after our time. If our time isn't producing good works, we must reevaluate ourselves. Social networks are great for communication and reconnecting, but we must remain disciplined. We must be the boss. We must not lose power to anything in our lives that takes control of our precious time.

When we give away our time to idle pursuits, we give away our Christ centered confidence to vain consumption with an endless appetite. Row, row, row your boat gently down the stream. People row their boats gently down the stream... to where? Nobody knows or cares as long as there is entertainment on board. To give too much time to unfruitful activity is to lose trust in the God who produces fruit in our lives. Trust is built in relationship. Relationship requires time to develop that trust.

God gave us a story to be told. We must continue to be intentional in sharing what God has done in our lives in all circumstances. This God given assignment is personal.

Nehemiah didn't hide or run from duty when others discouraged him, questioned him condescendingly, lied about him, and threatened his life. His attitude was, *"I am doing a great work and cannot come down. Why should the work stop while I leave to come down to you?"* (Nehemiah 6:3, AMP) This was a rhetorical rebuke! He was responding out of his vision statement. It was clear that not all the people understood.

Not everybody is going to understand the desire to bring everything to completion, and they don't have to. It is between you and your Lord. We are accountable to Him; be confident in that. The prophet Jeremiah says, *"[Most] blessed is the man who believes in, trusts in, and relies on the Lord, and whose hope and confidence the Lord is"* (Jeremiah 17:7, AMP).

Discouragement produces resolve in our faith, and opposition refines our mission.

Nehemiah wasn't just building a wall; he was building a bridge to gather God worshippers who had been scattered all over the earth to turn and come back home to the Lord. Nehemiah was building a bridge large enough for a generation of people to come back to their God. He wasn't only concerned about himself or even the present generation; Nehemiah was building legacy. His concerns were for other Israelites to honor God and implant those values in the family bloodline. Nehemiah didn't pursue the vision alone. He brought other people with him and assigned them tasks to carry out. That's how he shared the vision, causing the Israelites to become stewards of the vision to restore

Jerusalem. Completing the mission will inspire the people who are most dear to us.

Do you see the confidence in Nehemiah? Does he sound arrogant? There is a fine line between arrogance and confidence. Confidence draws people towards the vision and arrogance causes people to dismiss the vision. Confidence comes from continually trusting in the Lord, and it is His Spirit that draws people towards that character. Arrogance is the trust we have in ourselves, bringing pleasure to ourselves. This only seems to perpetuate that arrogance. Proverbs 28:26 says, *"Those who trust in themselves are fools..."* (AMP)

If we believe God had us begin something, we should believe He will finish it through us. We don't need to ask God certain things, because we already know His will by His Word. But it is important to determine in the beginning of an endeavor if God wants us to do it. We need to know God's mind on the subject, and this comes through His word and personal relationship.

> *But He is unchangeable, and who can turn Him? And what He wants to do, that He does. For He performs [that which He has] planned for me, and of many such matters He is mindful.*
>
> —Job 23:13–14, AMP

God describes Himself as the Alpha and Omega, the Beginning and the End. God said through the prophet Isaiah,

> *Declaring the end and the result from the beginning, and from ancient times the things that are not yet done, saying, My counsel shall stand, and I will do all My pleasure and purpose...*
>
> —Isaiah 46:10, AMP

To make it easier on us to be involved in God's purpose, we should see a vision of the end product. It will make all the bumps in the middle feel like part of the journey rather than a roadblock to discourage us. Remember God has declared the end result and His counsel will stand.

I have fought the good fight, I have finished the race, I have kept the faith.

—2 Timothy 4:7, NIV

Paul's first day of work for the Lord started with a reproach. He was blinded, with no guarantee he would ever recover his sight, and immediately questioned by his new Boss, *"Why are you persecuting me?"* (Acts 9:4, ESV) The proud Saul was led by the hand like a child into Damascus and neither ate nor drank for three days. Welcome to the ministry, Saul. By the way, God just changed your name to Paul. I hope you like it?

Yet Paul went on to change the world! Paul passionately proclaimed the gospel to the nations and their kings. Inspired by the Holy Spirit, he wrote thirteen of twenty-seven books of the New Testament and eventually had the courage to be martyred for his faith in Jesus Christ, whose people he once persecuted.

The apostle Paul wrote 2 Timothy in the latter half of his ministry, indicating that struggles come when serving the Lord. He declared victory over those struggles by staying in the fight and keeping the faith. Paul finished stronger than when he began.

I used to play competitive ice hockey and people often asked me, "Why do you guys fight?" In hockey, if you don't stand up for yourself once in a while, then every time you have possession of the puck, the other team mentally believes they can take it away from you as they please. If you're not willing to push back, the opposing team takes liberties that affect the outcome of the game.

If you're not willing to fight in life, your spiritual opponent will think he can take that which you have possession of at will and with little effort. Our common enemy will fight even though he's already defeated.

In order to finish certain tasks, we must stay in the fight. We cannot take a neutral position on the battlefield. We must take a critical position that awards the upper hand to those who possess it! Christ has secured our victory, but we still have opposition. Even the angelic messenger who was dispatched to Daniel, in Daniel 10, was delayed twenty-one days until Michael, a chief prince angel, arrived to help the mission succeed.

Just because we have to endure for a cause doesn't make it any less godly. We must be able to stand up against all the strategies and deceits of the devil. The devil would like us all to be acquainted with a pattern of giving up. We do not contend with physical opponents. These struggles are not all as they appear. We must engage in all that the crisis demands so we may stand firmly in our faith, drawing our strength from Him who provides might without limit.

Small matters can have big consequences. To mankind, small matters have small results; to God, small matters can have bigger implications. All we have to do is stay in the fight because Christ has won.

As believers, we aren't just survivors. We don't look for ways to barely get by unscathed. We are over-comers. We don't fight to defend what Christ has already won; we engage to move forward and establish the Kingdom of God here on earth. Yes, sometimes it gets ugly and we're left with scars to prove the battles we've been in, but self preservation should never be an excuse to retreat in our daily journey.

chapter ten

FIND THE WAY THAT PLEASES GOD

A FRIEND OF MINE WHO TEACHES HIGH SCHOOL WAS GIVEN APPROVAL FROM the administration to give his entire class an A before they ever stepped into his classroom. What high school student wouldn't run to that class?

The course studies meaning, truth, and areas of knowledge. Students are allowed to think critically, respectfully disagree with other's opinions, and challenge one's own assumptions. The students require a safe learning environment to be able to communicate their ideas, change their minds, and engage with others whose perspectives are different.

An A reflects a job well done and removes the pressure that comes from an individual's personal performance and fear of failure. The advanced grading fosters truthful, insightful context and creates an atmosphere independent of popular generalizations.

That freedom leads to discovery. It's an expression of the grace of God to love and accept—and yes, give us an A—before we do any works for Him. We are not accepted by what we do or what we plan to do, but by what Jesus Christ has done by the love of God. God appreciates honesty expressed from sincere hearts. Sometimes our nature wants to disguise the true condition of our heart with complacent motions that require attendance, accomplishments, and counterfeit motives. In other words, image becomes more important than sincerity.

As a result of the automatic A, from the beginning these students have the freedom to engage, be creative, and discover what's really in their hearts. The atmosphere is unpredictable, fluid, and introspective.

The students need a mature, confident teacher to guide them securely into the exploration of their own beliefs, so those admissions are revealed from the heart and not the head. Students don't have to write assignments to please to their teacher, but are able to investigate internally.

God has already given us an A based on the assignment of His son Jesus Christ, who handed in the work on time when He said, "It is finished." Grace was given before any of our works were accomplished. This gives us the liberty to explore who we really are, who God really is, and what He is capable of doing in and through us. There's no need to hide our condition behind a mask because we've received our exceptional passing grade. We are safe to explore in the Kingdom of God.

When that liberty is given we have room in our hearts and minds to love, be innocent, and seek God for the way in which He wants us to engage every matter. God wants to be our God in every moment. We can be honest with ourselves when we are disappointed, God is still our God and He still has a perfect plan. The truth is we just haven't figured it out yet!

> *...so that you may live a life worthy of the Lord and please him in every way: bearing fruit in every good work, growing in the knowledge of God...*
>
> —Colossians 1:10, NIV

There's a way to do everything. When we surrender our ways to align with His ways, it will bear fruit, good works, and growth in the knowledge of who He is. That increasing knowledge of God seems to perpetuate good fruit in our lives that please Him.

David inquired of the Lord, "Shall I go up against the Philistines? Shall I pursue the band of Amalekites?" As imperfect as David was, he is still most often described as the man after God's heart. The Amalekites had kidnapped two of David's wives, and he still bowed down and asked God, "What is your way?" David never overestimated his own ability to discern the will of God. Nor did he jump to replace the will of God with human reasoning. Two of David's family members were kidnapped while he was out and he didn't immediately pursue the Amalekites like emotion would have demanded. Instead he took the required time to see which way God wanted him to proceed, and the Scriptures report that he recovered all when he obeyed God to pursue the Amalekites. Nothing was missing. In fact, David increased his holdings by capturing the Amalekites' flocks and herds.

There is a free will choice to go about accomplishing certain tasks, and most people operate according to consequences rather than communication with God. What grants the greatest results with the least amount of effort? We've been trained through repetitive exercise to problem-solve this way.

Our conditioned response, mixes with our natural personality, on a pendulum of caution to ambition. This human programming leads us to not explore outside our box of experiences or understanding. God is much bigger than our understanding.

> *...don't try to figure out everything on your own. Listen for God's voice in everything you do, everywhere you go; he's the one who will keep you on track. Don't assume that you know it all.*
>
> —Proverbs 3:5–7, The Message

Assumption causes us to only partially commit. We presume to know that this is the way it should be done, but subconsciously not with absolute confidence. We speculate regarding His will because it is more convenient and comfortable to guess at what God is doing rather than get down on our knees. In return, we lack total confidence in the process because we lack total submission.

Didn't Moses make the same error when he struck the rock a second time instead of speaking to it? Our old nature is to rely on experience and human reasoning to fulfill our duties and then marvel at how close we are to God. This is the danger of assumption. We think we are right, but we can be entirely ignorant of God's will in the matter because of personal analysis. We figure out what God should do, then we pray. Or we share with God our understanding in prayer and give Him option A or B to fulfill our desires.

Faith and assumption are entirely different things, though they look similar. With faith, items are tangible in the spirit but invisible in the natural. With assumption, our desires are visible in our natural human logic and no faith is required.

Do we know God or do we just know what to do? Which reaction is greater in crisis? Society judges us by our conduct so we lean on the importance of our response, but God searches deeper into our hearts to look at the motives of our actions.

Those who are in the realm of the flesh cannot please God.
—Romans 8:8, NIV

But without faith it is impossible to please and be satisfactory to Him.
—Hebrews 11:6, AMP

Amazingly enough, the famous roll-call of faith in Hebrews 11 doesn't bring up some of the Old Testament mistakes of these "men of old." Instead it illuminates the faith that pleased God.

[Prompted, actuated] by faith Abel...
—Hebrews 11:4, AMP

This doesn't mention the competition and tension between the brothers, Cain and Abel. I'm speculating here, but if I were to read between the lines it seems that these brothers, like many brothers, competed for attention and approval.

When the brothers' offerings were presented to God, He asked Cain, "Why are you sad? If you do well, will you not be accepted?" Cain assumed his fruit offering would be good enough for God. Cain's offering was self-righteous, because he had devised his own way to offer worship. It seemed that Cain's offering to the Lord was a burden to him, and he expected a blessing like his brother. However, Abel was also born into a sin nature; he likely wasn't blameless in his behavior towards Cain. In typical sibling rivalry, Cain was upset at God but took his frustration out on Abel. Cain and Abel both made offerings to the

Lord. Abel made one that brought more pleasure to God because he offered God's way with a blood sacrifice.

> *[Prompted] by faith Noah...*
>
> —Hebrews 11:7, AMP

This doesn't mention that he got inebriated and stripped down in front of his family.

> *[Urged on] by faith Abraham...*
>
> —Hebrews 11:8, AMP

There's no mention here of Abraham's moments of doubt in God's plan, or that his initial response to Sarah being pregnant was laughter, or that he slept with his servant Hagar as a way to perform God's promise with his own rationale.

God spends more time boasting about what they did well rather than what they did wrong, because that which pleases God will have a more lasting impact. God focuses more on what pleases Him than what displeases Him. When we adopt this attitude about ourselves, of seeing what we're doing well as opposed to what we're not doing well, we can live lives of faith and gratitude. Not that we ignore our sin nature, but that we acknowledge more often the transformation that has taken place in our hearts to encourage ourselves and balance our self-image.

These men, despite their setbacks, weaknesses, and mistakes, found a way to please God through faith. Their testimonies are relevant today. In spite of self, they still pleased God. According to the inspired written account of the Holy Spirit, these men's trust for God overshadowed the times when they fell short of the glory of God.

> *So we make it our goal to please him...*
>
> —2 Corinthians 5:9, NIV

We face many choices and we don't always make the right decision. However, our intentions should be to find a way that pleases God in all circumstances. Sometimes we don't really get a choice; things just happen and we don't have time to choose. We still must find a response that pleases God, remembering that motives of the heart are more important than outcomes and actions are rewarded greater than intentions. If our goal is to please Him, the execution is not what brings pleasure as much as the humility of our heart.

To bring pleasure to God, we live by a faith that is unhindered by our thoughts. Faith is raw, uncalculated, and even appears reckless. Faith is the long game, not always expressed properly in a moment but over many moments before, during and after an event. Peter denied Christ after the Lord prayed his faith would fail him not, and still he went on to recover and strengthen his fellow believers throughout the Book of Acts.

Faith is different from ambition, assumption, and analytical conclusion. Faith is preparation, expectation, and satisfaction. Faith will change us before it changes our situation.

Faith is more crockpot than microwave. The microwave heats up the food but reduces the taste. The crockpot also heats up the food but emphasizes the natural flavor that is already present. The crockpot takes more preparation and time to cook, but the outcome is a higher quality and you feel better about your choice. Faith is measured over time. God has plenty of time to do a work properly in us. Yes, we trust God, but do we *still* trust God?

The disciples in the boat with Jesus, while He was sleeping, shouted in a panicked state, "Don't you care that we are going to die?" Jesus arose from His nap, *"rebuked the wind and said to the waves, 'Quiet! Be still!'"* (Mark 4:39, NIV) When we don't see Jesus working for us right away, we think that all is lost and God doesn't care. Jesus then turned to his disciples and said, "Where is your faith?"

Even in turmoil, when we long to turn our attention solely on ourselves, or in situations when the outcome doesn't seem to matter to anyone or anything else, we can find deeper meaning if we search it out. Ephesians 5:10 says, *"And try to learn [in your experience] what is pleasing to the Lord [let your lives be constant proofs of what is most acceptable to Him]."* (AMP). God doesn't skip the process or attempt to speed it along, but He doesn't slow it down either. His timing is a direct reflection of who He is. He is perfect in every way.

Navigating our lives by all that we see can be misleading to those who desire to live by faith and be led by the Spirit. We need to develop our personal relationship with God and apply His Word to tap into our spiritual senses. Those spiritual senses reveal the truth, affirming God's will more clearly.

The people of God walk by the truth in the Word of God, not by what they can touch, smell, and see. They have accepted God's Word as reality over current events. They find ways to please God in all that they do, remembering that small steps of obedience pays dividends in God's greater design.

chapter eleven

3G NETWORK

I MET A MAN IN GERMANY WHO CHANGED THE WAY I THINK IN MY LIFE BEFORE
I ever came to faith in Christ. I was visiting a castle during a wedding
reception when I saw a girl I had met earlier marching towards the
exit with a hammer in her hands surrounded by her friends. It was like
watching a mother duck lead her ducklings across the street.

"What's going on?" I asked her.

She stated that she had locked her keys in her car and was going
to break the window to get them out. I convinced her to let me see if
I could pop the lock before she smashed the window. I did manage to
pop the lock and was able to retrieve her keys without harming anything, so that evening I was the hero—for that group of people anyway.

When I returned to where I was staying the next morning, the
owner of the house had heard about how I was able to get the keys from
the car without any damage. He repeated the story as he had heard it
and asked if it sounded right. My response was yes. Then he said something very surprising to me: "Give the glory to God."

What? What did that mean? I didn't get it, but I remember saying
to myself, after trying to decipher the significance, *Okay God, have the
glory.* I seemed okay with that decision. It actually felt like the right
thing to do.

From that day forward, I desired to interpret everything in my
life that turned out well to determine if God should get the credit. I

realized that there was something more behind this man's statement than just those five simple words telling me to give the glory to God.

So then, whether you eat or drink, or whatever you may do, do all for the honor and glory of God.

—1 Corinthians 10:31, AMP

I acknowledge God's hand upon my life in all that I do now. I operate on a "3G" network: G*ive the Glory to God*. We cannot always see 3G, 4G, or LTE networks actually doing the work they were designed to do, but we definitely know if they work or not. Technicians could describe a more specialized explanation of how computers around the world share information, but even those educated people wait by faith to see if the theory will actually work. The internet is essentially a WAN (wide area network) that covers the entire world and has the ability to provide all people with the same knowledge.

We cannot always see God actually doing the work, but we can all testify to the work He has done and is doing behind the scenes. This network of His glory makes the power of the internet less impressive, because though the internet can make life easier, it will never have power to give life. God's glory can speak to all mankind simultaneously, no matter one's location or language, and is more reliable than any internet connection.

The young minister Stephen is described in Acts 6:8 as being *"full of grace (divine blessing and favor) and power (strength and ability), working great wonders and signs (miracles) among the people"* (AMP). The next verse states that some members of the synagogue began to debate in disagreement with Stephen, but they were unable to resist the intelligence, wisdom, and inspiration of the Spirit with which, and by whom, he had spoken. The Spirit of God was operating in this vessel and the glory of God was shining through him for the others to see. The nature of God was on display for all to witness.

In desperate response, the members of the synagogue plotted to accuse Stephen of blasphemy against God and had him falsely arrested.

As he stood before the Sanhedrin council, arrested on bogus charges, the very men who were to judge Stephen gazed upon him intently and saw *"that his face had the appearance of the face of an angel"* (Acts 6:15, AMP). The glory of God glowed from him as he stood in front of earthly judges.

In Acts 7:1, the high priest asked Stephen, "Are these charges true?" His response to being falsely accused was *"Brethren and fathers, listen to me! The God of glory appeared to our forefather Abraham…"* (Acts 7:2, AMP) Stephen testified for the following forty-nine verses on how God revealed His glory on earth to the Israelites, the same horde of kin who had just indicted Stephen and was about to pass judgement on him. Stephen didn't defend himself and ask for mercy. Instead he glorified the Defender and Merciful One.

> *But he, full of the Holy Spirit and controlled by Him, gazed into heaven and saw the glory (the splendor and majesty) of God, and Jesus standing at God's right hand.*
>
> —Acts 7:55, AMP

Stephen was full of the Holy Spirit and saw Jesus standing, not sitting, at the right hand of the Father. Stephen had the glory of God beaming through him, and Jesus, in His glorified body, recognized and acknowledged him. Glory recognizes glory! This is one reason why we give glory to the Glorious One, so we can experience Him in supernatural encounters to strengthen our faith.

We need rain to make it rain again. There needs to be enough moisture in the atmosphere for a downpour to take place. As we give God glory, He brings us deeper into the familiarity of His glory.

Can you imagine Jesus seated in splendor, His eyes searching the entire earth, looking to and fro for a human vessel who reveres God and has allowed the Holy Spirit to control him? The glory of God, Jesus Christ Himself, notices Stephen and arises from His seat at the right hand of the Father to certify that the acts of the Holy Spirit through this submitted servant had indeed glorified the Lord.

Standing is a position of honor and respect. We are members in good *standing*. When we applaud with admiration, we give a *standing* ovation.

Even everyone who is called by My name, whom I have created for My glory, whom I have formed, whom I have made.

—Isaiah 43:7, AMP

We were created to be spectacles of His glory here on earth, like Stephen. In other words, our purpose is to praise God, worship Him, proclaim His greatness, seek Him, and accomplish His will on earth. When we give Him all the glory, His glory shines through us, perpetuating His glory on earth.

This is what glorifies Him. God has given us a reason for our existence, a meaning for our lives. We were created by Him, according to His desire, and our lives are to be lived for Him so that we might accomplish what He has set for us to do.

Jesus is the tangible glory of God. The introduction of Jesus to mankind on earth declared the glory of God at His birth.

Then suddenly there appeared with the angel an army of the troops of heaven (a heavenly knighthood), praising God and saying, Glory to God in the highest [heaven]...

—Luke 2:13–14, AMP

Hebrews 1:3 classically states that Jesus is the radiance of God's glory and the exact representation of His being, sustaining all things by His powerful Word.

The glory of God is all-encompassing. Wherever we go, whatever we do in life, remember that God can make an exhibition of His glory through us. As long as we are present, an ambassador for Christ has been deployed by the Lord God Most High. It doesn't matter what arena we're in. Take responsibility that your presence will glorify the Lord and behave accordingly.

There is no need for an undercover secret agent. Be an ambassador; they drive around in luxury rides with the flags of their country so all will know who they represent. Let us showcase the glory of God and allow God to intervene in the challenges we face daily, to the amazement and wonder of all the bystanders.

Let people recognize whom we belong to not by physical flags, but by the glory that exudes through us. Let His glory be our mark of distinction.

Growing up on the farm, I learned some things about the harvest season. Sleeping is inconvenient but necessary. Eating gets in the way, but we probably should do it. Kids going to school is a hassle, but I suppose they should get their education. Harvest is not priority number one; it is the only priority! There is no second priority until the mission is finished. Everything else is of secondary importance. Basic needs are bothersome. We must realize the season that we are in and the type of meaningful work we were custom-created for. The power of the Holy Spirit that dwells in us is not for our benefit alone, but for God's glory, to be presented to the world as it awaits the return of our Lord Jesus Christ.

Whatever field we find ourselves in right now, we need to work in His harvest! If every servant in the body of Christ took up this attitude with passion, there would be no place on earth to hide without encountering the glory of God.

Consider the locust in Proverbs 30:27: *"The locusts have no king, yet they go forth all of them by bands"* (AMP). A locust by itself is hardly noticeable and of no threat, but a band of them going forth is a cause for alarm.

Locusts seem to understand that apart from unity they are helpless. But if all these creatures made in similar likeness act upon the same vision, hoping for the same outcome, even the most powerful nation in the world can be brought to its knees. Just ask the Pharaoh of Egypt! Alone they are merely pests. Together, operating in unison, they become a plague! God is able to use details that seem small to us to highlight His glory. We take care of the small steps of faith in our lives and God will ensure the bigger plan is achieved.

When Nehemiah and his team finished Jerusalem's wall in fifty-two days, all the enemies of Israel heard of it.

When all our enemies heard of it, all the nations around us feared and fell far in their own esteem, for they saw that this work was done by our God.

—Nehemiah 6:16, AMP

Nehemiah was able to bring different types of people together in one heart and one mind to work for His glory to be a spectacle for all to see.

We are all in this together with a common purpose. Kingdom minded people work together to see the glory of God on display. Ego and insecurity is made small through teamwork to elevate the One who deserves the recognition. We need our 3G network to operate all over the world so the revealed knowledge of His glorious attributes may demonstrate His divine plan for mankind.

The daily anthem of ours hearts must be to give God the glory, to exalt Him exclusively for His proven faithfulness, love, grace and righteousness, to acknowledge His holiness, sovereignty, majesty, and power. He alone is worthy of our enthusiastic praise, and our eternal salvation can be found nowhere else except through His Son Jesus Christ.

chapter twelve

BATTLES IN THE VALLEY WE MUST WIN

For the Lord your God is He Who goes with you to fight for you against your enemies, to give you the victory.

—Deuteronomy 20:4, ESV

GOD IS THE ONE WHO GOES WITH US, EVEN IN THE DAILY GRIND OF LIFE. WE have to stand against every mental doubt, physical barrier, and spiritual foe to appreciate God's victory in life's battles. We still have to go to the combat zone even when family isn't with us, friends cannot support us, and the world doesn't understand us. God said that He is the one who will go with us and defeat our common enemy.

Some fights we cannot lose. I'm saying we win by simply engaging our enemy with God's word! Sometimes we can't afford to roll over and die, or just go away, even though it would be easier. Moses had to go back to Egypt. David had to defeat Goliath in front of his doubters. Joseph couldn't stay in self-pity, the pit or in prison. Peter had to come back to his senses. Christ had to rise again! He was never meant to stay! They all had to confront an obstacle to their purpose through an unpleasant confrontation.

An inferior force wins when the superior force doesn't show up. Once we possess Christ, sin no longer reigns, but sin still wages war against us. The pressures and cares of this world will attempt to throw yokes around our necks to enslave us and stop us from the liberties of living in Christ. People who are at war look for ways to win.

Battles in the Valley We Must Win

There are some situations in which the outcome really does feel like a matter of life and death. No other person can engage in these battles for us. We have to go to our contest armed with the only One we really need.

As David said to Goliath in the valley of Elah,

> *And all this assembly shall know that the Lord saves not with sword and spear; for the battle is the Lord's, and He will give you into our hands.*
> —1 Samuel 17:47, AMP

The Bible says that David ran to the battle line. The sword and spear are physical weapons made by the hands of man, but God doesn't give victory by favorable odds. David had no training in weapons of warfare, but he had the radical belief that he would prevail because God was with him. David stood alone in this fight.

His own father Jesse disqualified David as a contestant to be king when the prophet Samuel asked all of Jesse's sons to be present for the choosing. David's eldest brother Eliab, whom David was anointed with oil by Samuel in front of, tried to discourage David in the battle against the Philistines by mocking his insignificance. When Goliath publicly challenged the army of Israel, they all fled from him terrified. David witnessed trained military men refuse to fight because of fear. A scene like this doesn't reinforce the idea of fighting Goliath as practical.

King Saul himself spoke disheartening words to David as he volunteered to fight, telling him that he wasn't able to win against this champion. Even the enemy scorned and despised the audacity of this adolescent for even bothering to appear before the great Goliath.

It seemed that David's personal achievement was merely getting to the battle; the God of Israel provided the public victory.

We may have to stand alone in a season of life where it appears that no other person on the planet remotely understands what we're going through. But take courage, because if God has delivered us once He will come through for us again. David was delivered from the mouth of a lion and a bear and given no reward, but his confidence from those

89

events established his boldness to believe in God's deliverance from the Philistine giant and receive a great reward.

> *But our way is not that of those who draw back to eternal misery (perdition) and are utterly destroyed, but we are of those who believe [who cleave to and trust in and rely on God through Jesus Christ, the Messiah] and by faith preserve the soul.*
>
> —Hebrews 10:39, AMP

During my competitive hockey days, I recall skating into the corners of the ice thinking that there is no way that anybody but me is coming out of that scrum with the puck. My opponents could be bigger, they could be stronger, and they could even outnumber me, but I knew that the player who believed he would come out of the corner with the puck was the one who most often did. The longer the skirmish went on, the greater chance of success I had because I knew I would never give up.

The longer a battle ensues, the better our resolve of faith will be established in us. The battle is for our benefit and the exaltation goes to God. The greater the garrison built by satan to prevent us from moving passionately forward after God, the greater the blow will be to the deceiver when our personal courage in the dependability of Christ succeeds. The longer the fight, the more savory our victory! Our faith in the final outcome grows every second that the battle delays.

Struggles don't give us permission to give up; they are part of God's plan for our lives. Waiting to see victory is not a curse, but an expression of God's perfection. The more time we take to prepare, the more He provides. It is an expression of His glory. God takes one shot and knows He will not miss! David only needed one smooth stone to kill Goliath though he had five.

Why do we wait at a red light when we want to get through the intersection? We expect it to turn green. Our foot remains on the brake for safety as we wait in the ready position. Red lights are there for our safety, but as soon as the light turns green our foot moves from the waiting position and nudges down on the accelerator. Our necks strain a bit as our head bobs. When it's time to go, we know it's time to go! We don't need to be told to go. When we wait with anticipation, our eyes fixed on the signal, we never miss.

It takes time for us to move forward safely. We are not the only drivers on the roads. God orchestrates the entire intersection so that the timing is perfect.

Let the challenges in life assure us that God is at work behind the scenes, aligning everything according to His purpose. Some of His best work is done in the backdrop. His brooding is His preparation.

Why don't we eat mac and cheese right out of the box? It's not prepared! All the ingredients are present in the package, but they're not ready. Is it possible that our noodles are a little too tough? Maybe we haven't spent enough time in hot water. Perhaps the milk and butter still need to be added to make us a little more smooth and textured. Or maybe that delicious cheese-flavored powder hasn't been added to us to give a distinct flavor. Perhaps we need some salt to purify us, to make us a little more enjoyable to digest. People might even come back for second helpings appreciating the quality time put into the dish.

God didn't say that He will go on your behalf to fight your enemy, He said that He goes with you to the fight, fights for you, and gives you the victory. The fight may put us in hot water but we shouldn't lose hope. We're just being tenderized. We need to simmer a little bit.

Sometimes we've got to deliver a message, no matter how clumsy it is. Sometimes we've got to set a standard and not walk away. Sometimes we've got to shout, dance, laugh, cry, or sit in silent peace to get out of our regular tendencies. Sometimes we've got to offer, serve, believe, move on, or look foolish. Sometimes we've just got to take a stand against the enemy knowing that God is with us.

Even now, take your stand and see this great thing which the Lord will do before your eyes.

—1 Samuel 12:16, NASB

We've got to make our position known to all principalities.

You will not need to fight in this battle. Stand firm, hold your position, and see the salvation of the Lord on your behalf...

—2 Chronicles 20:17, ESV

We've got to ready ourselves in a fortified stance.

Put on the full armor of God, so that you can take your stand against the devil's schemes.

—Ephesians 6:11, NIV

We've got to defend what we believe to be true about His Word.

Some battles we must win by refusing to withdraw, stand our ground, and believe His Word regardless of our circumstances. We must know that God is with us. In our darkest day and deepest valley, we must remember that God is a God of the valleys, too.

My second daughter, Laurel Joy (LJ), was born around 8:00 p.m. The doctors had warned Andrea and me of possible complications, but we were people of faith and knew that nothing, by no means, could harm us or our family. We believed with every fiber that our LJ would be fine despite the doctors' warnings.

Everyone close to us began to pray when Andrea went into labor. We were calling down every heavenly tongue believing God for a miracle baby, beating the odds. Nurses, doctors, and attendants would walk into the room, see us in deep intercession, and not interrupt. I reminded God of every scripture about children, every personal promise He had made to me in close fellowship.

Even when Andrea's water broke, I still believed that LJ would be fine.

Laurel Joy came into this world perfect to her parents. She looked so much like her sister. She was sweet, warm, and small. Laurel squeezed my finger and let out a few baby sighs.

Laurel left this world three hours later, at 11:11 p.m., but she changed our lives forever. We held Laurel until 5:00 in the morning and she had turned cold to the touch. I couldn't convince my muscles to twitch enough to turn away from my baby. I kept saying in my mind that it was time to go, but my body wouldn't respond. I couldn't turn my back on my daughter. It was my duty to protect her and watch over her, and I would have given my life to that end.

I was helpless. I was in shock. I, who was so confident in my faith, who calls himself *Favor* in the spirit, had my world turned upside-down. I asked God, "How can you ask me to go through this?"

God responded, "I can ask you because I also lost a son."

At that moment I knew that God was there with us. I remembered the covenant He has made with His people. God's Son Jesus is seated at His right hand; they are together again. One day in eternity, I will join my precious, perfect daughter to embrace her as I did in our limited time on earth. I still cry when I think about her, but I also still stand firm in my faith.

Tomorrow has no guarantees. Some people will tell you that they'll live to be 120 years old. I will not live here that long. There isn't enough time here on earth to tolerate defeat. Losing LJ was the hardest day of my life and the most difficult season of my life. If the devil finds you going down, questioning God, he doesn't release the pressure. Instead he administers a crushing squeeze, hoping we will finally give up.

For the rest of that year, a lot of devastating news came to our family and we had to withstand a lot of heartache. I was tempted to say to God, "How much more of this can we take?" But I remembered what He had said in the labor room and I recalled His covenant and promises—that our lives are not played out in a single season. God goes with us to fight our enemies, and even when tragedy strikes He is faithful to be standing at our side.

Instead, after some time, I found myself asking satan if he'd had enough, not because of pride but because of the strength of the One who stood with us in the battle. Circumstances made us weak, but our faith made us unbreakable. We understood the gift of life on earth and the gift of eternal life after earth. The more adversity we stood through, the stronger in our convictions we became. God uses personal suffering to bolster our faith in the blueprint of His design for our lives. It's one of the mysterious ways in which He works, one of the methods that makes God's ways not our ways.

Those events that don't seem fair in life lead us to discover just how immense God's long term plan is for us. When we stand in the valleys of life, where victory seems hopeless, we must remember our promise and recall our training, when we defeated our own lion and bear, like David did, when no one else was around.

chapter thirteen

EXCELLENCE THAT SEPARATES

I WANTED TO EXPRESS MY LOVE TO MY WIFE ONE DAY, SO I CHOSE TO TAKE on a challenge I was uncomfortable with. I chose to make her favorite dessert—a lemon meringue pie—from scratch. Yes, I could have gone to the bakery, purchased one, and told her that I loved her and was thinking of her. She would have appreciated it. I would have been comfortable with that and the outcome would have been positive.

Baking the lemon meringue pie was a different story. I had little to no experience in that department, but I wanted to show her that I had taken the time to teach myself, take a risk, and go way out of my comfort zone. I looked up a recipe, purchased the ingredients, gathered my baking tools, and began. (You know that anybody who calls them "baking tools" is unqualified to complete this task.)

I learned that day how to make a lemon meringue pie, but I also learned something about excellence. You see, even though my wife hadn't even tasted this pie, it was already excellent. I took diligent steps to express my genuine love and would accept nothing less than my best effort. I acknowledged my inexperience in baking to Him; I left the result in God's hands and Andrea loved it.

God has trusted us with a mission and for the slothful it is difficult to interpret. Excellence means more than doing the best you can. Excellence is doing your best under God's supervision, with His resources, which raises the standard beyond your personal best.

When people don't do well at a task, the reason is often a lack of something. "I didn't have this, I didn't have the knowledge, I needed a team around me..." People excuse mediocre outcomes with lack of resources, but the determining factor is often the measure of trust in the Source. God will provide His resources and knowledge to the project. If we invest, God will invest. God is a team builder and participates in the process when He is included.

Our minimum standard should be what others would consider excellent, because of our access to Him. Look for ways to improve the outcome. We should endeavor to gain a reputation for doing tasks well. If we don't critique ourselves, we leave it to somebody else to assess. Even God turned around to evaluate His craftsmanship. In Genesis 1:31, God saw all that He had made, and it was very good.

> *But let every person carefully scrutinize and examine and test his own conduct and his own work. He can then have the personal satisfaction and joy of doing something commendable [in itself alone] without [resorting to] boastful comparison with his neighbor.*
> —Galatians 6:4, AMP

Those who scrutinize their own work don't feel the need to seek further compensation by competing against others. We compare ourselves to others when we trust in our own ability. Is this why our parents, coaches, and mentors we respect later in life are the same ones who said to us, "Try your best. That's what counts"? They wanted to remove the pressure of us finding acceptance only through good results.

Excellence doesn't compare itself to other people or things. Our results aren't always a reflection of how great we are or how great we aren't. God has the bigger picture in mind. Some arrangements fall under His sovereign will, and God doesn't need us to defend His honor by giving an explanation for everything.

Excellence is best measured in the execution of a work—not always the return. Too many uncontrollable factors come into play to assess by payoff alone. Apart from His empowering grace, we can do nothing of eternal value. We must foster a culture of humility with our capabilities and consider the measure of God's grace assigned to us in any given season. We cannot fabricate results. The human desire for affirmation is too strong. We can't ignore the temptation for pride to embellish the outcome of our works when our concern is self-promotion as opposed to the indefectible work of the Holy Spirit.

Excellence is in the heart behind our decisions. God isn't after the conclusion of the matter as much as the obedience and submission of the heart during the matter. This is why our faith in God allows the outcome to be God's alone.

True faith produces excellent works. Excellence is not the absence of problems; it is the process of eliminating problems through trusting ourselves less and the Lord more. If we simply lay down our expectations before the Lord in prayer and let Him lift up the conclusion in His ways, the spirit of excellence will function through us.

At the time when Jesus was crucified, do you think all involved were saying, "This is an excellent work"? No, because their standard was the standard of common people. They thought His death on the cross was a disaster. This is why the disciples scattered and Peter denied any involvement. Our hero Jesus did not save us by a mediocre work at the cross; we were saved by an excellent work. Nobody would have said that at the moment of crucifixion, but after the resurrection all could declare how powerful the cross was.

Let our faith be our guide to be excellent in all that we do. Excellence is not a series of good decisions, but rather the surrendering of our own will and glory. It is the passionate pursuit to eliminate every hindrance from the manifest glory of God, to put on display His glory through rudimentary people. God's excellence radiates through those who can leave their reward at the altar as an offering, because our reward is nothing compared to the warm embrace of a Father who quietly whispers, "Well done, good and faithful servant."

Daniel was distinguished above other leaders because of the spirit of excellence upon him. His competitors could find no fault in him because he was faithful. Daniel 1:8 says, *"But Daniel determined in his heart that he would not defile himself by [eating his portion of] the king's rich and dainty goods or by [drinking] the wine which he drank"* (AMP). He was committed and loyal to the cause, despite his own discomfort.

The cost of excellence was to deny instant gratification and comfort. Daniel wasn't guided by his flesh or peer pressure, instead he yielded to the spirit of God which produced the excellent outcome.

Excellence correlates with a person's obedience to God. Show me a person with an excellent spirit and you will also show me someone who responds in obedience to the will of God. God is the source of excellence. We don't know what our sovereign God is going to do, but we know that God works out everything in agreement with the counsel and design of His will.

Daniel didn't modify his beliefs to accommodate the local culture, nor did he accept the luxury offered to him by the king. He kept God's purpose and route clear in his heart. The Bible says that he *purposed* in his heart. The purpose behind a motive directly affects one's measure of excellence. When we have impure motives, it seems like everybody sees them except us. We all get uncomfortable when someone makes small talk with us as a prelude to asking for money. When our motive is His purpose, His excellent spirit comes upon us to rise above mediocrity.

Daniel made a decision first in his heart that he wouldn't accept the king's meat. Can you imagine the other candidates? They may have thought, *What's the big deal? Oh well, more for me! Are you too good for us?* Was it worth all the hassle? Daniel had already determined not to compromise on his convictions.

A divide appeared among the group. A separation took place, and separation seems to be a requirement for excellence. When we choose to separate ourselves from the crowd for God, God separates us from the crowd through an excellent spirit.

Elizabeth was filled with the Holy Spirit and declared to Mary the mother of Jesus, *"Blessed are you among women, and blessed is the fruit of your womb!"* (Luke 1:42, ESV) Mary's womb was blessed among all women's wombs. Her womb was separated. Mary's assignment to raise our Lord Jesus Christ was an excellent work.

Paul was separated from the other Pharisees and Christian persecutors on the road to Damascus so he could carry the gospel to the gentiles and go on to write much of the New Testament.

The twelve disciples were separated from the crowd. David was separated from his brothers when he was recruited by Samuel. Joseph was separated from his culture. Job was separated from his blessings. Jonah was separated from civilization. They all went on to do an excellent work.

We ourselves have been called out from the world and into the family of God to do an excellent work. Plan to have an outcome that exceeds the mediocre, then implement the plan in prayer. God will do the rest.

Therefore, my beloved brethren, be firm (steadfast), immovable, always abounding in the work of the Lord [always being superior, excelling, doing more than enough in the service of the Lord], knowing and being continually aware that your labor in the Lord is not futile [it is never wasted or to no purpose].

—1 Corinthians 15:58, AMP

True, consistent faith and resolve produces excellent works. When excellence is expressed through the divine and human partnership, an attribute of God is revealed. Excellence is the manifestation of God through man and the representation of His character.

Being excellent is to surpass ordinary standards, to excel, rise above, and have preeminence. It is an attribute that separates God from man.

O Lord, our Lord, how excellent (majestic and glorious) is Your name in all the earth!

—Psalm 8:1, AMP

What attribute is attached to your name? Think of somebody you know. A friend, a coworker, a fellow student. Now, what is the first adjective that pops into your head? How would you describe them knowing that nobody else will ever hear it? Lazy, impatient, hardworking, honest, loud, trustworthy... we naturally attribute adjectives to describe people in our minds. Attributes are attached to our names.

Know that other people have done the same regarding you. Perception always starts out neutral, until you reveal your character. Be faithful to the process God designed for your life and the spirit of excellence will be attached to your name in all that you do.

chapter fourteen

PRIVILEGE AND SACRIFICE

SOME SEASONS IN LIFE ARE TOUGH TO GET THROUGH. THEY PUSH US FURTHER than we are willing or ever expected to go. They may require more prayer, more sacrifice, more time, more attention, and more patience.

Some tasks feel never-ending, worthless, confusing, and unappreciated by God and His people. In some duties we are mistreated, betrayed, manipulated, and unnoticed. God uses those circumstances in our lives to teach us about Him, because we cannot run far away from those situations and still be able to hold onto Him.

At one stage in my journey, my church was renting a facility to host our Sunday morning meetings. We were fortunate enough to purchase an old warehouse in the middle of the city to transform into our new meeting place.

This manufacturing warehouse had had the same tenants for twenty-seven years and had clear evidence that they'd worked hard in steel fabrication. To be kind, it didn't look anything remotely like what you'd think a church today should look like. Steel beams, concrete, industrial equipment, grime, and posters of provocative girls scattered all around. Plenty of signs of a work-hard-party-hard lifestyle.

The senior pastor asked me to oversee the conversion of the building. The next three years of my life would be consumed by this assignment. I bought a truck to transport my tools, pick up material, and deliver goods so I could save the church money. Andrea taught herself how to draw to scale so she could design the blueprints that she saw in her heart. The slogan among the team was "We have no money, no time, so get it done well." We were indirectly saying, "Only God."

I would renovate all day. At night, I researched how to oversee a building project while negotiating with contractors. I called in many favors from my network, soliciting donations, volunteers, and discounts while holding myself accountable to the standard God had put in my heart.

Many nights after the volunteers left, I worked by myself in that dark, cold, dirty steel building, cutting concrete or digging holes for plumbing, all in secluded heartache because I honestly had no idea what I was doing. I had no experience, limited knowledge in commercial construction, and felt the weight of responsibility with all eyes watching to see if this would actually work. Many people more qualified than I told me that things couldn't be built the way I planned to build it. It *felt* like the other half was telling me it should have been done this way instead, but only after we had already completed it. I say it *felt* that way, it was not always so, but when you feel overwhelmed it is easy to become discouraged.

I suffered. I was tired of having to discern who was telling the truth among the contractors, and who was trying to rip the church off. My family suffered. I was working at the church late most nights while my daughter was growing up. I served full-time as a pastor in the church, ran a business to pay the bills, and became a commercial contractor for the Lord.

The question I heard over and over again: "When are you going to finish so I can...?"

My body was falling apart. I had tendinitis in both my arms and had about forty percent mobility in my neck. I rarely slept. I gained twenty pounds because I wouldn't stop working, thinking, and planning. I survived on fast food. People were kind enough to point out that I was getting overweight and looking tired. Didn't these people see that this was costing me and my family so much?

The hard truth was that I wasn't enough. I lost sight of the Source. All of my resources, creativity, determination, and commitment were not enough.

My team and I were building the church while God was doing a work in me. He broke me down physically and emotionally until I cried out to Him.

Near the end of my commitment to the project, as we were about to receive full occupancy from the city, the Lord said to me, "You are not good enough, but Christ is more than enough. This building project is the most honorable service you have ever provided." Christ was constant through my three years of specialized servanthood. I was the weak link, yet my service was honorable because of what it cost me.

Only someone who has sacrificed more than you ever could can speak to a person that way. My ability and determination was wrestling with God's supernatural strength and provision. I had become so weak that God needed to put me back together, and I gladly acknowledged the need for renewal in my life.

God let my tank run dry before bringing me relief. He needed my full attention to remind me that even admirable servanthood must be born out of, and remain in faith re-enforced by, the divine strength of God. God was more concerned about my heart than my production.

> But when the kindness and love of God our Savior appeared, he saved us, not because of righteous things we had done, but because of his mercy. He saved us through the washing of rebirth and renewal by the Holy Spirit, whom he poured out on us generously through Jesus Christ our Savior, so that, having been justified by his grace, we might become heirs having the hope of eternal life. This is a trustworthy saying. And I want you to stress these things, so that those who have trusted in God may be careful to devote themselves to doing what is good. These things are excellent and profitable for everyone.
>
> —Titus 3:4–8, NIV

The building taught me that our greatest sacrifice is our greatest privilege. What costs us most is what becomes our proudest distinction. Ask any parent who is involved in their child's life. They'll tell you about the selfless act of raising a child: changing diapers, making sure they eat well, helping with homework, and taking the time to explain to them appropriate behavior and expectations. Sleepless nights, hospital trips, parent-teacher interviews, volunteering at school, rides to every club practice... It's a lot. And yet, with the smallest advancement in their personal growth, we forget everything it cost us to support them. The reward far exceeds the cost. That is why it is our privilege.

Many days, we feel like no one else cares or notices. We feel like we're not advocating change in anyone's life, so why bother? We feel like we aren't making a difference for the Kingdom of God. We feel marginalized, unappreciated, and misunderstood. Our desire to promote the welfare of others comes from God who saved us through the washing of renewal by the Holy Spirit. If we trust in His grace, have the hope of eternal life, then we can devote ourselves to doing what is good with genuine intention because His promises are profitable enough to carry us through.

As servants of God, we shouldn't be putting a spotlight on our outward accomplishments and reminding God of all we've done. We should bring our achievements to the altar of God as an offering. Through the process, reminding our human nature that it has a tendency to seek praise for what we have done because of pride.

We must yield our minds, bodies, and will to the direction and guidance of the Holy Spirit. This preserves our energy, protects our relationships, and keeps the glory flowing upward—to Whom it belongs.

We should be producing fruit that is expressed outwardly of what the Holy Spirit is doing inwardly. We cannot simply pray for it to come out. Since this fruit is produced by the Holy Spirit in us, we must be able to admit who we are not, so He can change us into who He wants us to be. The by product of that process is spiritual growth and maturity.

Speak the truth to yourself. The lack of truth leads to a lack of trust in God. When we can't admit our true condition to ourselves, it is an expression of not being able to trust Him enough to change us. We know that something is wrong. To not self-evaluate is to deny ourselves. If there is more to be accomplished, why would we not reach for it? Because of fear and pride? Either we don't believe that God can produce more in us or we believe that God has already produced more than enough in us. Both outcomes are a symptom of unbelief. What is born in the flesh, the Spirit will not carry. The energy we need to fulfill what we are faithful with comes from our expectation and trust in the Lord.

David wrote, and I paraphrase, "[M]y zeal for God and His work burns hot within me" (Psalm 69:9).

It's not really what you do that makes you a servant; it's the motive behind what you're doing. If your motive isn't based on your love and appreciation for God, it's the wrong motive.

Some are motivated by recognition, promotion, and position. Others feel guilty or obligated to serve somewhere. They misunderstand that somehow good works will bring more acceptance from God. Sacrifices made with a reward in mind creates unmerited expectations of some kind of compensation that will never come.

True servants who are motivated by the love of God always stand the test of time. Servanthood isn't something you can retire from. Servanthood isn't something you grow out of or move on from. It's in the heart. Servants aren't afraid to discuss their weaknesses, because they always want to draw closer to God and live with a broken heart before their Lord. They meet needs. They have a heart of understanding. They listen carefully and see further because they feel like if there's an opportunity to be a blessing, they want to be on the frontline of that. Servants don't wait to be asked. Christ didn't command His disciples to serve; He lived a life worthy of imitation and they followed the pattern through observation. His life is still worthy of imitation today.

The apostle Paul said, *"Let each of you esteem and look upon and be concerned for not [merely] his own interests, but also each for the interests of others"* (Philippians 2:4, AMP). He went on to say that we should have the same attitude toward one another that Jesus Christ had. The Kingdom of God needs to come first, before all else. Sacrifice is the expression of the life of Jesus. His death on the cross is His greatest mark here on earth. How many people will you see today that wear a cross on their body or around their neck?

People are remembered for what they endured for the welfare of others. We set a day aside to acknowledge the men and women who serve our country in the military.

Only Ever

Servants are submitted to God above all. Submission is in our attitude. Servants must be compelled by love, not reward. The privilege of sacrificing our lives in servanthood towards God is life's greatest honor. To express the pure motives of a servant is to exercise service toward people who can never pay you back. Perhaps they won't even acknowledge or appreciate it, but then you can acknowledge that your own motives are for the right reason—love.

chapter fifteen

CLEARLY COMPASSIONATE

THERE ARE MANY CONTROVERSIAL TOPICS TO DEAL WITH AS MODERN-DAY BIBLE believers. Society is slowly loosening its hold on God's word as a guide. Frankly, society is moving further from biblical principles aggressively and will continue this trend for some time. As this darkness spreads, pockets of light become more intense. God will cause His church to shine more brilliant with truth and power. However, we still need to be able to interpret our environment in all conditions.

Sexual identity is being rationalized with God's love for everyone. Euthanasia is defended by free will choice and individual autonomy. If a woman was violently raped, should she be allowed to have an abortion? If this child will only remind her of the worst day of her life? Most people reading this likely have taken a firm position. These are speculative subjects to provoke thought and open discussion. Many of us bypass this process to arrive at our conclusion. It's imperative to believe in the absolute truth of God's word, but what about the people who have not yet had their lives renewed? How do we relate to them? How do we relay the message of hope that has saved us?

We are all aware that God's Word is our standard. We should face these complicated affairs rather than quickly stone someone with judgement by avoidance and rejection. We should open our hearts to the Spirit and be moved by compassion to demonstrate God's love for them. Jesus died for them, and no matter the ambiguous situation, one element is clear: Jesus died for our sins and rose again to give us hope in eternal life with God!

There are several examples in Scripture where Jesus was moved with pity and compassion.

> *When he saw the crowds, he had compassion on them, because they were harassed and helpless, like sheep without a shepherd. Then he said to his disciples, "The harvest is plentiful but the workers are few."*
> —Matthew 9:36–37, NIV

Jesus recognized their condition, but He didn't go into judgement mode. Instead Jesus acknowledged the state of being and saw the deeper need. When He witnessed distress, hurt, and suffering in people, He said that they are like sheep without a shepherd and that the harvest is ripe. Compassion must motivate the body of Christ, just as it motivated the Head of the Church, Jesus Christ Himself.

We are on this earth today for these same people. These conditions are a result of their separation from God, who knew them in the womb as well. God makes it easy for us to see who needs a Savior. Homosexuality, strife, and witchcraft don't send you to hell; separation from the one true God does. All people are in need of grace.

The love of God is clear. Our present mandate is not to judge people. Judgement will never change people, only bind them. We are challenged to love the ones who reject, repulse, and rebut us. Let the Holy Spirit convict and transform people. That is what He does. Our mission is to express the love of God. Let the people around us see the fruits of the Spirit in our lives.

Loving people is easy to do inside the church walls, with people who agree with us. We cannot build safe shrines and only send out invitations with directions on them; we need to build bridges upheld by love and acceptance, take people by the hand, and walk with them in the Lord—not just to church. When they discover the love of Christ, He will compel them to come. It is an invisible work that we don't have to fully understand.

It is very damaging and out of touch to paint a broad stroke over somebody's beliefs and, without having a relationship with them, say, "You are an abomination to God." That is incorrect. People are not the abomination; their sinful nature causing certain behavior is the abomination.

We should remember that many of these beliefs have been a consistent pattern throughout their lives. People are deceived and judgement won't open their minds, but love will. Some people call it speaking truth in the hopes of awakening reconciliation, but it often fosters rejection and causes the already wounded to become more so. Narrow is the path that leads to life but it doesn't mean our understanding has to be narrow as well. It's like saying, "Here, enjoy this egg. Eat it entirely. No breaking the shell to see what's inside and no preparation time allotted for cooking."

The sinful nature we inherited as a species is what causes separation from the Father.

While we were yet sinners, Christ died for us. A liar is not different from a pedophile. Christ offers the same redemption for both. All can be accepted as right-standing sons and daughters in the Kingdom of God.

Jesus revealed Himself to the Samaritan woman at the well. In doing so, He stepped outside the Jewish boundaries. First, He spoke to a woman; Jewish men did not speak to women in public. Second, she was Samaritan, a group the Jews traditionally despised. Third, He asked her to get Him a drink of water, which would have made Him ceremonially unclean from using her cup. Some people would have judged Jesus as a sinner in today's church. It was offensive to the religious.

The Samaritans were a mixed race people who had intermarried with the Assyrians centuries before. They were disliked by the Jews because of this cultural mixing, and because they had their own version of the Bible and their own temple on Mount Gerizim.

To add more depth, the woman was in sexual sin, a transgression that is easy to pass judgement on. Imagine the public attitude towards the sinless Son of God, who came down from heaven, engaging in fellowship with an adulator! How repulsive to bother the Holy One with this unholy one. Whatever You do, Jesus, don't look at her! She might contaminate You!

This was not the disposition of Christ. It is not the pattern Christ gave us to follow.

The woman at the well came to draw water during the hottest period of the day, instead of the usual morning or evening times, because she was likely rejected and scorned by the other women of the area because of her immorality. She wasn't proud of who she had become. She was probably ashamed, isolated, alone, and guilty. Society had rejected her. Her sin had separated her even from other sinners.

Do you know anybody who fits this description? I do. That was me before Christ.

Yet God chose to reveal His loving nature to her. Jesus didn't say, "Don't you know the Ten Commandments?" He didn't pull out His superiority. Instead He said, *"Whoever drinks the water I give them will never thirst"* (John 4:14, NIV). He was speaking of eternal life!

That should be our concern and our stand. How can we use situations to reveal the love of God to His creation?

It's interesting that while the Jews and Sanhedrin refused to believe in Christ, devising ways to discredit Him and His disciples, the Samaritan and her people received and accepted Him. The harvest is ripe when we are willing to go out to the field.

Jesus Christ isn't just for those who have already found Him! He isn't just for the local church, as He wasn't just for the Jews at the time. He came to give life, hope, and to seek the lost!

Be clear and compassionate. The speed at which society is eroding is alarming, but God's Word, His plan, and His mind have not changed. Grab onto the stability of the infallible attributes of the One who demonstrated to us how to maneuver this life.

One of the challenges in the twenty-first century is that we are inundated with knowledge and opinion. It's so readily available and so unverifiable. Intellectual pride rampantly exerts pressure on the church to dilute God's Word with the knowledge of man.

Paul wrote,

See to it that no one takes you captive through hollow and deceptive philosophy, which depends on human tradition and the elemental spiritual forces of this world rather than on Christ.

—Colossians 2:8, NIV

At one time we may have followed the ways of the prince of the air, and even though his spirit is at work in those who are disobedient to God, we must not be seduced by our surroundings. Instead we are to be a beacon of light representing the only option to receive salvation.

Our pop culture is entangled with deceptive bait. One modern social scientist refers to culture as integrated learned behavior patterns. We accept as truth how we see other people consistently behave. People become our standard. We walk by what we see rather than what we believe in God's Word.

So how do we navigate through this life dealing with the influence of popular lifestyles? These systems of human behavior are evil in their fallen nature. Not the systems themselves, but mankind's proclivity to erode moral standard, which is celebrated in pop culture. Avoiding or living in denial is not a solution. Culture doesn't exist without people, so it cannot corrupt us apart from encouraging personal rejection of Jesus Christ.

These systems are vehicles that the deceiver of mankind has infiltrated to mix a little confusion in with truth, just enough for us to question, "Can what God said really be true?" Satan's first words to mankind. The most subtle and crafty creature, with a one-liner strong enough to cause the fall of mankind.

Listen, I don't believe satan chose to barrage Eve first because she was a woman. In fact, she didn't have a name yet. She was referred to as "woman." Eve wasn't yet called "life spring," as her name means. Perhaps she hadn't yet identified herself. Eve didn't yet understand how God saw her. She didn't know who she was, whom she belonged to, and what she already had access to.

Many of us often face the same challenge. We are not sure where we stand in all the messages of the world. If we don't know who we are in Christ, we are easily persuaded into rebelling against the Word of God! Can what God said really be true?

Perhaps another reason Eve was the first target is that she had received her instruction secondhand. Who hasn't referred to Google when they have a medical symptom? We believe unverifiable opinions. It's hardwired into our DNA to search out answers to problems. God built us this way to naturally seek a solution for our sins.

In Genesis 2:16, we learn that only Adam was present with the Lord to receive the direct instruction not to eat from the tree. Eve received the directions from Adam, but the predicament arose in their miscommunication of God's words.

In Genesis 2:17, with only Adam present, God says, *"[Y]ou must not eat from the tree of the knowledge of good and evil, for when you eat from it you will certainly die"* (NIV). Okay, that seems clear. But in Genesis 3:3, the woman repeats the instruction this way: *"You must not eat fruit from the tree that is in the middle of the garden, and you must not touch it, or you will die"* (NIV). Somewhere along the way, some misinterpretation brought confusion.

Confusion spawns deception. When we live apart from the purity of His Word, the father of lies sets traps of deception through all possible streams of influence.

> *...for God is not a God of confusion but of peace...*
> —1 Corinthians 14:33, NASB

Nobody will hear God's instructions the second time like we hear it the first, but are we willing to pay the price to go treasure hunting? Are we willing to go into unchartered and uncomfortable territory seeking the fortune of God's revealed Word?

The Bible was written for more than just the church. It was written to reveal the truth of God's plan so the world could choose. We cannot pretend we are from a superior tribe of morality. Retreating to the home base of the church doesn't ensure ground will be won for the Lord, nor does it provide safety for long. Jesus never remained in the synagogues, though He loved and lived off of every word spoken by His Father.

We have to be clear on where we stand, for our own sake. The world is seeking authenticity. Compassion for people dying spiritually should motivate us to swim into the cold waters of sinful humanity to rescue another heart of flesh. This is a clear mandate in God's grander scheme for people of faith to entwine in their everyday life.

chapter sixteen

TRUST, THEN CHANGE

WHEN THE MUSIC CHANGES, THE DANCE NEEDS TO CHANGE, TOO. IN A metaphorical sense, the deejay (God) is unchanging, but He plays a variety of music throughout our lives. Some music is energetic and we've got to praise Him; some songs are more ballads, evoking internal inspection, and we enter into deep prayer; other songs speak of love, meaning it's time to slow dance with the Lover of our souls in worship.

Whatever the music playing, our movement should reflect the melody to maximize our personal growth and usefulness in the Kingdom. If we are able to surrender our will, God is able to change us.

Familiarity opposes our faith. We feel more in control of our affairs, but expose ourselves to diminutive maturation. Change is an expression of faith. Many of us don't feel ready to draw too close to God because we know He will put His thumb on our hearts to change in some areas. So we remain in a long-distance relationship, hoping for His benefits without total commitment.

And do not be conformed to this world, but be transformed by the renewing of your mind, that you may prove what is that good and acceptable and the perfect will of God.

—Romans 12:2, NKJV

When a person renews their mind to discover God more deeply, God is able to change their identity. Change is the evidence of an encounter.

God will sometimes go one step further and change a person's name to help establish them in their new identity. The new name is the mark God leaves behind to remind them of the divine revision.

God appeared to Abram in Genesis 17 and renamed him Abraham, and his wife's name changed from Sarai to Sarah. Saul changed to Paul during his encounter on the road to Damascus, Simon changed to Peter, and Jacob changed to Israel. These encounters were an intense exchange with the Lord. As people they were transformed and their names followed suit.

People who sincerely change can be trusted because they have been in the presence of God. A person who has been corrected and disciplined by God is a person you can count as faithful. These are people who can adapt to the movement of the Spirit despite what popular opinion and culture dictates.

The culture you grow up in affects the way you live the rest of your life. When you grow up with an accent, you don't know it's an accent until you meet other people who don't sound the same.

When the Israelites were captive in Egypt, their culture developed into a defeated, oppressed, slave mentality. They had no hope. It's difficult to point fingers at a nation that had been methodically broke down for over 430 years. When you only see what slaves see for that long, it's difficult to change perspectives. Difficult, but not impossible.

Joshua and Caleb endured the same hardships. They heard the same stories passed down from their fathers. They surely had days that seemed never-ending and hopeless as Egyptian whips forced them to labor on. However, these two also witnessed the miraculous deliverance of Jehovah at the Red Sea, along with the rest of the Israelites.

So what was the *"different spirit"* (Numbers 14:24) upon Caleb that distinguished him from among the others?

In Numbers 13:2, the Lord instructed Moses to send twelve men into the land of Canaan. Joshua and Caleb were the two notables among the twelve.

God was looking for covenant. God wanted His chosen people to see the promise, to catch the vision for themselves. God was sending a leader from each tribe, likely because He knew people would be apprehensive.

Later in Numbers 13, Moses instructed his leaders to bring back fruit of the land as evidence that the promised land was plentiful.

> *"How is the soil? Is it fertile or poor? Are there trees in it or not? Do your best to bring back some of the fruit of the land."* (*It was the season for the first ripe grapes.*)
>
> —Numbers 13:20, NIV

Notice the last sentence of that verse: *"It was the season for the first ripe grapes."* The grapes were about to break through. The environment was ripe with hope for the breakthrough. When God shows a promise, the atmosphere is ripe for us to believe that the vision will be brought to pass by the Lord, if we are willing to seize it by faith despite past cultural conditioning.

Promises must be born into our conscience first. Our conscience is a delivery room. God doesn't force dominion over it. It's a place where we must surrender to Him. If the promise cannot be perceived there, how will we grasp it by faith? God doesn't regulate whether good or evil thoughts are produced there. That's why it is imperative to take every thought captive in obedience to Christ.

We must see the unseen. There are two ways to see. The more common is to see something and believe it. Our physical environment convinces us of the reality of what we've just witnessed in chronological time. The second way to see, which is less common, is to believe something and then see it. Our faith, or spiritual environment, convinces us of the reality of what we've just witnessed though it has not yet passed in chronological time.

So after forty days of inspection, the scouts returned to give a report based on the facts they witnessed with their physical eyes. The scouts showed the land of Canaan's fruit and brought word saying that the land was flowing with milk and honey.

So what caused the death of a generation that came out of a defeated culture? Unbelief. Refusing to change their minds and embrace the promises of God by faith despite witnessing firsthand the miracles of God in Egypt and at the Red Sea.

In Numbers 13:28, the Israelite scouts described the people who lived in the land as strong, though they didn't engage them to test their fighting skill. They gave account of impervious cities that were large and fortified, though in all probability they had no experience with walled cities, having grown up in Goshen, Egypt. They also spoke of seeing the sons of Anak, people of great stature and courage—again, courage being difficult to measure in a race of people. They fed doubt and discouragement throughout the community by making assumptions.

Speculation will kill belief in the promise God spoke. It is an enemy to faith. Speculation lets the mind wonder and embrace fear of the unknown. Fear promoted man's opinion above God's will and His ability to work in and through people.

Caleb, the gentleman with the different spirit, retorted, *"We should go up and take possession of the land, for we can certainly do it"* (Numbers 13:30, NIV).

Caleb, did you not see what the others saw?

To Caleb it seemed as though it was an empty land. His outlook was that they should possess the land as if nobody had any claim on it. Caleb seemed to understand that the longer the delay, the greater the doubt would become.

Procrastination is a belief destroyer. The further we go from a promise, the more difficult it is to rediscover that promise. Caleb was voracious, declaring to his brethren that God was able to eliminate every hindrance, that they could adapt to a new way of life despite the dominant cultural patterns they had always known. We must follow that example to fulfill the vision. We must not delay or waver in our belief.

His fellow scouts rebutted him, saying that the Israelites couldn't go against the people of Canaan because they were stronger than the Israelites. There you have a conclusive decision by majority. Diplomacy at its best. The annihilation of belief.

In order to take hold of our promise, sometimes we must go against the majority conclusion. It's often not the easy route, and it certainly requires more effort, but then again, narrow is the path that leads to life. People's approval doesn't ensure that God is in it.

Sometimes we must be contrary to popular belief in order to retain the purity of our belief. It's amazing that when we're not sure what to believe, everybody around us offers their belief in the hope of finding agreement.

Mankind is hardwired to operate on what we believe. As a man thinks, so is he.

On this day, a unanimous decision was not required to reach the resolution that the Israelites chose. Caleb and Joshua understood that a promise from God *is* the majority vote.

In Numbers 13:32, the scouts reported that it was a land that *"devour[ed] those living in it"* (NIV). That makes it sound as if even the land that flowed with milk and honey would destroy them.

All the people they saw in it, apparently, were men of great stature. No women? Children? It seems as if the physical size left a greater impression on these people than God splitting the Red Sea and swallowing the Egyptian army. The dangerous exaggeration of human reasoning convinced an entire generation that God was not enough.

In Numbers 13:33, the team of scouts said, *"We seemed like grasshoppers in our own eyes, and we looked the same to them"* (NIV). How the spies saw themselves is how the sons of Anak saw them as well? The essential function of a spy is to go unseen by the enemy. Unless these beliefs that the Israelite spies adopted were created in their minds through intimidation, not by actual interaction with the sons of Anak.

God isn't asking us to look the part to accomplish His will; He is asking us to trust Him without exception to bring His purpose to fulfillment.

At no point does God require their skill to improve, numbers to increase, or a clever strategy to be adapted. God desires to intervene on their behalf in response to absolute trust in Him.

The scouts had a small self-image because they saw their qualifications in themselves rather than in the likeness of a faithful God who is able.

I should qualify that. Ten of the twelve had a small self-image. Caleb and Joshua may have seen themselves as small, but they acknowledged that God is bigger!

In Numbers 14:2, the Israelites let their unbelief fill their hearts with discouragement and complained to Moses, *"If only we had died in Egypt! Or in this wilderness!"* (NIV) They probably wished they had been more careful about what they said out of discouragement, because it seems that their complaints came to pass.

The sad conclusion of this story is that everybody aged twenty years and older died in the wilderness, never seeing for themselves what God was willing to do, with the exception of Joshua and Caleb. The majority of them believed someone else's report but still suffered the same fate. We are accountable for what we believe regardless if the information is first or secondhand.

Imagine living only to die, to wander the wilderness knowing there is no more promise ahead. Unbelief is a painful pattern that robs mankind of the many promises of God. It is one way that we defeat ourselves.

Our hearts must remain broken on the Rock in order for it to be quick to change.

It is difficult to change when we give our attention to hindrances rather than promises, because we see no good reason to desire change. This is called unbelief and it makes our daily walk mundane and dims the vision we were designed to pursue. There is always more to God than what we see. A changed mind leads to a transformed heart, and God is pleased to show Himself to transformed hearts.

chapter seventeen

BE SURE TO LISTEN

MY MOTHER WOULD FREQUENTLY SAY TO ME ON MY WAY TO ELEMENTARY school: "Be sure to listen to your teachers." She knew I had a tendency to lose focus on the instructions I was given.

In this busy world with so much noise, it can sometimes be difficult to hear God's voice and be steadfast in obeying what we heard. One thing I know for sure is that He is always willing to communicate, whether it's through His Word, another person, imagery, dreams, or circumstances. It's not always the topic we want to discuss, but valuable information is still exchanged.

What we listen to today will shape who we become tomorrow. That is the power of a word. Words stay alive long after they are spoken. That's why when a person says a positive or negative word about us, we rehearse it over and over again. The word continues to affect us.

God speaks to us not because we were in the right place at the right time, and not because we are oldest or the youngest of our siblings. He speaks to us so we may confidently trust Him.

The boy named Samuel heard God speak to him as a child servant in the house of God. Samuel knew how to serve Eli, the head priest, in the temple, and the Word of the Lord was rare and precious in those days. God called Samuel, and the young faithful boy ran to his master to ask what He needed. But Eli's response was just the point God was making. Eli said, "I did not call you."

God, not man, was calling Samuel. Eli instructed Samuel to return to bed, and if he should hear the voice again he should respond with "Speak, Lord, your servant is listening." Not "I'm serving." Not "I'm sleeping." Not even "I'm ready." But "I am listening carefully."

Samuel grew to be a prophet to speak God's will for the nation of Israel. Samuel learned to listen to God before he learned to speak on behalf of God. God's discernment is our reward for listening when we would prefer to speak.

> *The Lord had said to Abram, "Go from your country, your people and your father's household to the land I will show you."*
> —Genesis 12:1, NIV

This was the calling of Abram (Abraham). A calling means that somebody is attempting to communicate with us. A voice is speaking to us. We are being sought out. Somebody has a message for us to receive.

The Lord called out to Abram and said, "Leave your country (culture). Leave your people (tradition). Leave behind the language, relationships, and familiarity of your own kind. Go from your father's household. Depart from the security and encouragement that your family has offered to you for seventy-five years." To make the instructions more intriguing, God wasn't specific about where he was to go.

> *[Urged on] by faith Abraham, when he was called, obeyed and went forth to a place which he was destined to receive as an inheritance; and he went, although he did not know or trouble his mind about where he was to go.*
> —Hebrews 11:8, AMP

Before he knew where to go, Abram had to leave behind everything he knew. Obedience shows God that we are listening carefully. Sometimes we have to be willing to let go of what is going well, something we've worked really hard at and are proud of, even when He is not specific as to why. Sometimes we have to let go in order to go.

The simple expression of obedience communicates to God that our lives are no longer our own. The Bible records where Abraham's thought process was, by saying that the directives didn't trouble his mind about where to go.

Abram had lived a lifetime by our standards, but God told him to basically reinvent himself in order to receive the blessings God had in mind for him.

Obedience preceded the promise! We're not always in the proper position to receive what God has for us, so He asks us to make some adjustments. He has the bigger picture in His mind for our lives and His blessings must be delivered His way.

Can you imagine working seventy-five years for the same company? A person would be very good at their job. They would be well respected and feel very confident in what they do. But picture that same person, who looks so accomplished on the outside, feeling like something is missing on the inside. Would they have the courage to step away from everything they know? Would other people understand? Would they think leaving that job was impractical? This wouldn't happen without every co-worker trying to talk them out of it. That employee of seventy-five years would have to try explaining to the other workers that he had heard a voice and must obey. The boss would want to offer them a three-month stress leave instead.

When Samuel was going to anoint Saul, he said, *"Bid the servant pass on before us"* (1 Samuel 9:27, AMP). Or in other words, "Let the servant go so we can be alone." Then Samuel said, *"[B]ut you stand still, first, that I may cause you to hear the word of God"* (1 Samuel 9:27, AMP). We hear God best when we get still first and less distracted by our surrounding.

Ultimately, we have to own our calling. Others will not answer to God for what we were entrusted. We have to hear and obey our calling from God. To hear, we must be listening. Everybody has ears, but not everybody listens with the same focus.

During my time serving inside the walls of the church, I did my shift behind the sound board, mixing worship music through our speakers. During or after the service, people in the congregation often approached me or my team to give us feedback. It wasn't uncommon to hear compliments and critiques about the same music set. All these people were listening to the same sounds at the same time with the same waves, but their interpretations of the mix varied. After some time of maturing in my service to the Lord, I didn't let feedback, positive or negative, affect the way I served.

I spent more time than anybody else in the church training my ear to hear the optimal sound for the glory of God. My ears were equipped to serve the Lord with all my heart. When we are specifically trained to hear, we need to trust our training. If our hearing has been disciplined to hear the voice of God through fellowship with Him, we need to trust that we will receive what God wants to communicate.

Other people will try to tell us what God is calling us to do, because they might think we don't already know. Don't let them replace the voice of God in your life.

When God speaks to us regarding His purpose for us, nobody else is present. Nobody can interpret God's voice for us better than ourselves. We cannot assume that someone else knows God's intentions for us. Purpose is too personal, it is between us and our Father, to be shared intimately in the heart. It is the revealed knowledge of Jesus Christ and His plan for our lives.

People can waste time chasing after what somebody else has told them or insinuated to them about their God-given calling. In the end they are frustrated, depressed, and lack belief in the promises and purposes of God. When we hear God share the plan with us, our faith and confidence to see it through increases, regardless of doubters.

The Israelites served the king of Moab for eighteen years, until they cried out to be rescued by God. So God raised up a deliverer named Ehud. Judges 3:16 describes Ehud making himself a sword with two edges. A sword with two edges is not a tool for cutting trees, but made with the intention of killing a king and delivering a nation. Can you imagine the sound of Ehud sharpening both edges of the sword in a secret place so as not to be discovered while in the occupation of the enemy? It was a time-consuming process. Ehud was preparing to respond in obedience to execute on the promise of deliverance.

As Ehud's plan of action began, he presented the monetary tribute to the Moabite king, and sent away the other servants who had helped carry in the payment. The Moabite guards would have searched Ehud for weapons but found no sword strapped to the side of his waist, where most soldiers carried their weapon. The Bible says that he was a left-handed man. At this stage in history, left-handed people were considered physically handicapped and often forced to use their right hands. It's possible that Ehud had a real disability in his right hand, which is why he was forced to engage with his left. Ehud was dangerous because of his weakness. Ehud let the Moabites assume he had no ability to inflict damage.

Ehud intrigued the king by telling him he had a secret to share. The king cleared the room, seeming to view the left-handed man as harmless. No threat to anybody. God's deliverer then thrust his sword into the king's belly with enough determination that the handle followed the blade into the body, thus leaving no evidence of the weapon to carry out as he escaped undetected.

Ehud was raised up by the Lord to do a work that he was unqualified to do because of his handicap, but his hearing heart or obedience made him trustworthy. This attitude allowed God to perform in spite of human competence. Ehud would have been sure that He'd heard God's plan to deliver Israel.

I'm not sure that Ehud planned to kill ten thousand courageous Moabites that day, but I do know that he expressed his trust in God by those hours spent hewing the sword, possibly with only one hand that functioned well.

We know better than any other person, institution, or culture what God has called us to do in the big picture. The truth is that nobody else has access to that place in our hearts where God has shared our calling with us, unless we allow them means of entry by disclosing it.

Jesus said, *"My sheep hear my voice, and I know them, and they follow me"* (John 10:27, ESV). In most cases, we trust God but we don't trust ourselves that we heard God. Jesus also said, *"Whoever is of God hears the words of God"* (John 8:47, ESV). If we can't believe ourselves that we heard God, then let's take Jesus at His word. To walk by faith and not by sight, we have to be bold, confident, and not trouble our minds with how this is going to turn out.

Remember: it is in God's interest that we understand His big-picture purpose for us. God's voice must be clear and unimpeded by other sounds. When God speaks to us, our receivers must not be interfered with. It is in those times of communion and fellowship with the Lord that His direction is most intense. Nothing outside intimate connection with God is worth the risk of missing precisely what the Lord is communicating to us. He has a plan for us and it is perfect.

chapter eighteen

TOMORROW'S PROMISE

THE VALUE OF A SEED IS NOT WHEN IT IS IN YOUR HAND, IT IS WHERE YOU leave it behind that maximizes its worth. Every gardener knows that a seed is small but can reproduce itself many times over. It needs to be planted somewhere, and it needs to die. Seeds are planted in faith and are expected to produce fruit in the likeness of its kind.

> *Now I commit you to God and to the word of his grace, which can build*
> *you up and give you an inheritance among all those who are sanctified.*
> —Acts 20:32, NIV

There is an inheritance that belongs to us by His grace. Sometimes we know that we have an inheritance but we don't want to wait around to be built up. We need to be built up to be able to handle what God intends us to do with our inheritance. We often quote the scripture that says God won't give us anything we can't handle, perhaps overlooking that this time of testing applies to a positive blessing as well as negative temptation. It is never God's intention to crush us; sometimes even the benefits from God can lead us into rebellion when we are not properly prepared for them.

I have witnessed many wonderful people with obvious leadership qualities, capable of doing a tremendous work for the Lord, abandon their post because the pressure of the situation was too much. A breaking down of one's will precedes the building up. In an attempt to preserve our will, people will remove themselves from the setting to evade the breaking down process from God.

We are consistently tempted by the image of our calling (or the benefits of God's calling) because it is challenging to remain still and abide in Him, when we are not presently enjoying the advantages of belonging to Him. These images don't come in the shape of a golden calf, but rather idolatry in the heart. Did the Israelites not get tired of waiting for God and build an image?

> *When the people saw that Moses was so long in coming down from the mountain, they gathered around Aaron and said, "Come, make us gods who will go before us. As for this fellow Moses who brought us up out of Egypt, we don't know what has happened to him."*
> —Exodus 32:1, NIV

The very gold used to manufacture the golden calf was the back pay for the Israelites' years of slavery. They didn't leave Egypt empty handed, but they were quick to offer their inheritance over to false gods.

When we're reluctant to trust God in His process, we express impatience. Trust is built over time. We don't trust strangers; we trust relationships that have a consistent pattern of truth. We need to walk the same pattern several times before we develop a path. Pathways lead us to where we need to be. They also take time to establish.

> *An inheritance hastily gotten [by greedy, unjust means] at the beginning, in the end it will not be blessed.*
> —Proverbs 20:21, AMP

Our hearts are constantly in danger of making the same offering as the Israelites, to the false gods of this world. We become tired of waiting on God, so we offer our skills, time, and attention to seductive forms of idolatry. We put our hope in business plans, people, governments, and institutions to provide solutions to the things we are believing for, because tangible answers alleviate our discomfort in the unknown.

Deficient trust in God creates false idolatry. Believers are all too often ensnared by the benefits that are byproducts of our calling. When we walk in God's calling, we will have the influence we desire, but if we embrace it out of a need for human affirmation more than fulfilling God's purpose, we are deceived. When we walk in God's authority and are serving in His plan, but privately long for that power so our egos feel entitled, it is pride and false idolatry. When we secretly think like this, our hearts aren't ready to be trusted.

It is possible that our calling will give us honor and respect from others, but it is dangerous to long for these benefits with impure motives. Many are not willing to go through the pruning process; they're ready to discard what God began in order to shortcut God's plan, therefore undermining and dishonoring Him. Many people cry, "Choose me, oh Lord," until they receive their assignment from God. Refinement comes with hardship.

If we aren't alert as servants, we can slowly begin to serve God for the affirmation of man instead of remaining organic in our service. We become polluted by flattery and acknowledgement. We find ourselves thinking that other people are ungrateful. Or perhaps we become disillusioned when we don't receive the enthusiasm we expect of people.

Often when we read the story of the prodigal son, we rejoice over his triumphant return. Surely this illustrates the grace of God. But have you ever stopped to think about the eldest son who remained to help his father? Perhaps he became a little self-righteous, but look at Luke 15:31:

"My son," the father said, "you are always with me, and everything I have is yours." (NIV)

The eldest son remained constant and received an increase.

God wants to trust us with His reputation for His glory's sake, but first He wants to purge impure motives so we can be completely confident and transparent with ourselves before Him in relationship. The purging process can take time, so it requires perpetual trust in the Lord.

Our inheritance is waiting for us. David asked, *"Is there anyone still left of the house of Saul to whom I can show kindness for Jonathan's sake?"* (2 Samuel 9:1, NIV)

When Samuel the prophet met Saul for the first time, they sat down to eat together.

> Samuel said to the cook, *"Bring the piece of meat I gave you, the one I told you to lay aside."*
>
> So the cook took up the thigh with what was on it and set it in front of Saul. Samuel said, *"Here is what has been kept for you. Eat, because it was set aside for you for this occasion from the time I said, 'I have invited guests.'"*
>
> —1 Samuel 9:23–24, AMP

God is looking out for us, and watching over the inheritance that belongs to us. Remember that this is His plan, not ours; He has more invested in His ways than we do. More eyes are on Him than on us, as it should be.

When the twelve spies of Israel were sent to scout the promised land, it is worthy to remember that they were chosen as leaders with influence and a good reputation.

Among those twelve chosen, two men stood out because of their report. Now, understand that they all observed the same thing. They all stood from the same vantage point. Every one of them looked with their physical eyes. But they did not all *see* the same. Ten saw the current events, and two saw the conclusion of the matter.

Trust in God sees the conclusion, not always the solution. Solutions can be adjusted, conclusions are absolute. Once we act upon our belief, God will undoubtedly bring about a solution, but the first response has to be initiated by us. Faith does not deny reality or difficulties; faith declares that the power of God is greater!

Instant obedience reduces the luxury of reasoning and seems to open the door to God's inheritance. Caleb saw beyond what his natural eyes were telling him and surrendered his being to uphold God's promise. Caleb saw the land as his inheritance from God and was not deterred by the strategic challenges of possessing it.

What we see leads us into our purpose in life. Willingness to expose ourselves to suffering correlates with the value we see in our inheritance. Caleb was willing to risk death and the annihilation of his tribe to pursue the promise he wholeheartedly believed in.

Imagine the talk among the twelve before they presented their report to the public? It is not recorded in the Bible, but I often wonder who among them let fear override their faith as they gathered intelligence in Canaan. Who among them were so close to their inheritance but let it slip from their grasp because they lost focus on the Giver of that inheritance? Their promise was just on the other side of what they feared. What force could be so strong to defeat these people before they ever engaged in battle? All they saw, with their natural sight, was danger in Canaan. When you observe events, remember that there are more dimensions to God than what you can physically see.

There's nothing common about a burning bush not being consumed, or being swallowed by a whale and living there for three days. God isn't bound by the natural like we are.

God was looking for covenant. God was looking for leaders of the tribes who would pass on the faithfulness of God's promises, people who would receive their inheritance by faith and teach the next generation to do the same. Covenant isn't just for us, but for the people around us.

> *But My servant Caleb, because he has a different spirit and has followed Me fully, I will bring into the land into which he went, and his descendants shall possess it.*
>
> —Numbers 14:24, AMP

Not only did God remark about the loyalty of Caleb, but his family, because of his steadfast trust in the Lord, received an inheritance. This is the plan of inheritance. It is meant to be a shared birthright. This is covenant. The God of Abraham, Isaac, and Jacob allows His believers to be a receptacle and transmitter of His blessing. It is a distinguished mark upon His covenant that not only do His people receive His promise, but those around them also share in the blessing.

Noah, Rahab, Abraham, David, and even the kid with five loaves and two fish blessed those around them because of the abundance of God. Can you imagine that boy growing up to tell that story a thousand times with himself as the central character?

> *For if the inheritance depends on the law, then it no longer depends on the promise; but God in his grace gave it to Abraham through a promise.*
> —Galatians 3:18, NIV

Our inheritance is not earned or measured by our sacrifice, rather it is accepted the same way Abraham received it.

> *If you belong to Christ, then you are Abraham's seed, and heirs according to the promise.*
> —Galatians 3:29, NIV

He received his inheritance by faith in God's promise, and his descendants receive their inheritance by faith in the same God. Abraham acts as a receiver and distributor even though the origin of the promise is God.

To put God's inheritance in perspective, the covenant made between God and Abraham is still as important today, because it is Abraham's descendants who must receive the blessings to perpetuate the promise and demonstrate God's faithfulness. As time continues to pass by, the promise increases by the sheer number of people affected by it, thus magnifying His faithfulness.

Keep your eyes on the broader inheritance that is awaiting you at God's designated meeting place and time. It will be easier to sow without restraint into the Kingdom of God daily. Others will benefit from your contributions through covenant; remember that you also have your portion set aside.

chapter nineteen

STAY THE COURSE, TRUST THE PLAN

I HAVE BEEN DISCIPLED. I REMAINED COMMITTED TO THE HOUSE THAT GOD sent me to. I am proud of the way I have conducted myself through the years in the church. I became a pillar in the church, carrying my portion of the weight entrusted to me. With every opportunity, I tried to understand the prototype of God's church and apply it to the place in which I was an engaged, serving member.

My family added to the church. We made great personal sacrifices for the church. We see the unique value in the local church. We served in this church with our whole hearts. I became familiar with the church as a living, breathing entity made up of diverse people. We did our part to build the church of God while allowing Christ to develop us. My relationship with the church is a big part of who I have become in Christ. My family and I can confidently say that we produced good fruit in the body of Christ. Still, during the thirteen years of loyal service we knew the day would come to pivot into an entirely different dimension leaving behind all we had worked hard to build.

My big-picture purpose was made clear in the small steps of obedience that were taken during my routine week, serving the Lord and building the Kingdom of God through the local church. The outlook of my calling was always global, but under no circumstances would I compromise vision and God's timing in my life. I didn't want to leave my assignment too soon or stay too long.

Either God does it all, or He does nothing. We all come into this world naked, relying on another imperfect human being to nurture us. Everybody begins here on earth. Everybody will pass from here and face judgement. He offers eternal life and is not insecure about His plan.

Christ must be displayed, not disguised. His message shouldn't be debased with begging. Jesus is not the one broken. We are the ones who have been given this honor to know Him. It is our pleasure to pursue Him and operate in His perfect plan.

We should be vision-driven. Family and vision, under God's guidance, are the inspirations worth engaging in God's mandate for life. Vision inspires us to keep moving while family reminds us why it's worthwhile to sacrifice all we can handle here on earth. This is the reason believers destined for heaven still remain on earth: to be spectacles of His glory, fulfill His purpose, and leave a divine legacy. To live without vision is to die hopeless. Our lives depend on us finding purpose. We don't have to push ourselves into action when we live by big-picture purpose; that vision pulls us into engaging in Kingdom matters every day. When we are pushed by a force, it is from behind us, such as our past. But when we are pulled by a force, it is by our God, who has gone ahead of us. God leads us through this journey when we see ourselves in a surrendered state of feeble strength designated for God's purpose.

I lived a life without vision before I met Christ. I abused my body and mind with drugs and alcohol. I would stay out late, get in mischief and sleep the next day away. I had nothing important to wake up for. I had no design to follow. I had no vision, and I was slowly dying. Where there is no vision, the people perish.

Vision is imperative to Christian growth. It inspires our love for right living. Vision becomes precise the more you hate what God hates and love what He loves. A clear vision provides energy and exhilarates our faith.

Not all people will believe in our vision, or that we're able to follow through regarding our vision, including people who are familiar with us. Distractions from our vision will push us side to side. Our past will draw us back. It will be much easier to let our purpose die, to be content with what is in our hands. We have to identify these problems and realize they are small challenges to seeing our big-picture purpose. Vision is inconvenient until we make a commitment to engage it entirely. Suddenly everything else apart from vision in life becomes inconvenient.

A tree isn't afraid to lose its leaves to the wind, because it knows how deep its roots run. In different seasons of life, the tree will look bare and empty, because its environment is not conducive to healthy growth. But that same tree in a different season will flourish because of the depth and health of its unseen roots. Our lives aren't played out in a single interval. Our lives unravel through many seasons.

Our environment changes and people change. God does not. He is faithful. Understanding His ways isn't a requirement, but trusting His ways are.

There comes a season in every life when we're ripe for a breakthrough. The atmosphere is alive with a cool breeze and a fresh spring scent. We're intuitive in our design to sense that juncture, when the first budding plant is about to show life again after a season of stillness. The first sign of a new season is the passing of an old one. When the grace of God for that opportunity is upon us, it's time to spring forward and take a leap of faith. Every person must take this leap to become acquainted with the next stage of their purpose, to be able to release what is familiar in order to embrace what is unfamiliar.

I recall receiving instructions on bungee jumping when I was in New Zealand at the Kawarau Bridge. The facilitator had already bound my feet and hobbled me over to the edge, where there were two secured handles so I wouldn't lose my balance before I was ready.

There I stood on the edge of a bridge, surrounded by beautiful mountains and rushing water beneath me, about to plummet off this well-built structure for the thrill of trying something I had never done before.

"I'm going to count down from five," the facilitator said. "You make sure you let go of the security bars completely before I get to zero. Then just simply fall forward."

I remember thinking to myself, *This is bungee jumping?*

The instructor knew it was my first jump and was likely trying to help me cope with common anxieties from attempting to convince your muscles to perform in a way that your logical mind can't compute.

Regardless, he began his countdown.

Five. I completely removed my grip from the security rails.

Four. That's it. I'm jumping.

I squatted down, raising my hands in front of me, and leaped out as far as I possibly could from the bridge. I wanted to jump before he got to three. I couldn't wait!

If there was the promise of a thrill, and I was ready safety-wise, then it was absolute torture waiting around for something to happen.

God is our place of safety. Wherever He is, I want to leap towards Him with all my might. Wherever He is, that's where I know I am safe.

I cannot describe to you what that bungee jump was like on the way down, rushing toward that river. It's not because of excitement that I can't describe it; it's because everybody should have their own experience. We all have our own jumps to make. We spend more time focusing on what we don't want to happen rather than how awesome it would be if something did happen. In this case, I didn't want to die, but my focus was on the payoff, not the risk.

God will not convince us that making that leap is safe for us. We can only trust that God is our safe place to leap toward. Just as parents cannot protect their children from everything dangerous in this world, there is no safer place than being held in the arms of somebody who's willing to die so we may live. Jesus has already demonstrated through the cross that He is willing to do so. There is no more secure place than in His arms.

God will not disappoint. He has a plan worked out ahead of our lives here on earth. Job says that He performs what is appointed for us.

Our big-picture purpose requires preparation that is not always pleasant, but His plan for us is still perfect. Even when our lives are inconsistent, He is constant.

Disappointments, setbacks, and loss exist in our lives to change us. These seasons cause us to reflect on what is really in our hearts. We will not naturally go deep until discouragement provokes us into it. This is the place where real faith grows apart from His benefits. We discover the real substance of God and process His intimate truths. God doesn't just want us to know Him as a Provider, but also as a Sustainer. These times aren't intended to defeat us, only to identify us as His. In these moments, we are stimulated to seek Him with more desperation and discover what awaits us in this life and the afterlife.

We must make the leap into the unknown. If we're more concerned about reputation, comfort, or fear of failure, we'll never take the risk and never receive the reward of the fullness of God. In order to enjoy the thrill of walking in our God-given destiny, we must convince ourselves to completely let go of the security bars that have provided safety in the past.

There is no greater honor or fulfillment in life than to know and serve Jesus Christ with your whole heart. We must trust the unseen more than what we see. We must trust the Spirit of God more than our knowledge gathered through experience.

There is always more to God. Try something new. Don't be a square person in a square hole, accepting an uninspiring life. Don't believe the lie that this is as good as it gets.

We take the responsibility, because we must give an exclusive account to God for our lives. People will hurt us, not believe in us, and not agree with us. Purpose will always have opposition. Yet God will still ask for an account of what we did. We cannot excuse ourselves.

We should be a little loud sometimes. We should be a little unreasonable sometimes. A little awkward and unpredictable. Perhaps we should shake when everyone else is standing still.

When we know where we're going with God, other people will help us make a way to get there. When you meet someone in a narrow hallway, once you communicate to them which side you will pass on, they will move for you. The same principle applies with the purposes of God.

God doesn't need to call us to the possible. We'll take ourselves there, so why beckon us? God didn't instruct Moses to bring a herd of sheep out of Egypt, but a nation! God didn't ask Noah to blow up an airboat, but to build an ark that would preserve mankind and every species.

We cannot let pride hold us back from chasing God. It is difficult to stand out and fit in at the same time. Destiny begins with a decision to pursue it. God designed us to engage in every day Kingdom activity to lead us into His greater plan. That process is a full part of His purpose for us. Though we live day to day in our faith, God has always and will always operate with the big-picture purpose in mind.

No matter where we are in this life—whether on earth, in heaven, or in hell—He is still the *only God ever.*

ONLY EVER

Jason E.P. Johnson
Author / Minister / Speaker

For information regarding
Speaking Engagements please contact:

info@jasonepjohnson.com

Website: jasonepjohnson.com
Instagram: jasonepjohnson
Facebook: Jason E.P. Johnson
Twitter: @jasonepjohnson

Andrea Joy
Recording Artist / Worship Leader

Website: andreajoymusic.com
Instagram: andreajoymusic
Facebook: Andrea Joy
Twitter: @andreajoymusic